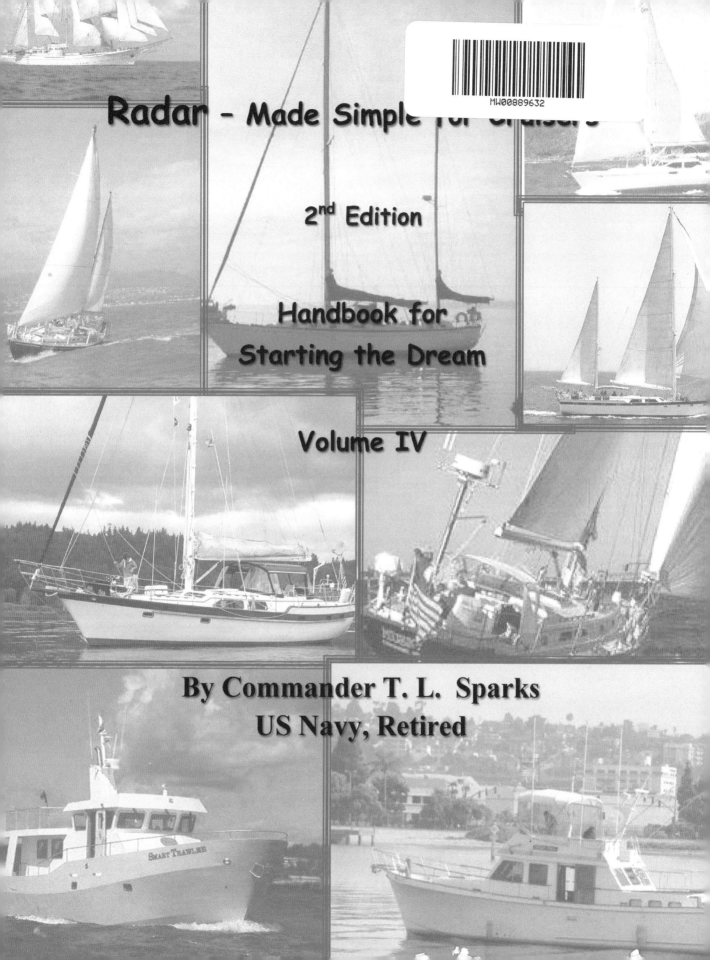

Radar - Made Simple for Cruisers

2nd Edition

Handbook for Starting the Dream

Volume IV

By Commander T. L. Sparks
US Navy, Retired

This book is dedicated to the memory of my son

Electricians Mate Second Class James Douglas Sparks.

September 5,1972 – January 29,1995

Pre word

Over the past few years cruising, I have run across a number of cruisers that take their life and ours in their hands every time they go out. So far those cruisers have been very lucky and their luck has resulted in myths about the need for radar on cruising boats.

Some of the myths that have developed and spread within the cruising community include:

Radar is not necessary
I have GPS and do not need radar
I am traveling with a group and they will help me
1. Automated Information System (AIS) took the place Radar.
2. It is not foggy in my area so I do not need radar
3. Radar is too hard to operate

This book will first address the myths and then explain how to stay smarter and safer with Radar.

Throughout this book the following terms are used.

> Return – The energy picked up and displayed on the radar display.

> Contact – A signal returned and displayed on the radar display that may be identified as another vessel.

> Vessel – A boat, ship, barge, or any other object actually moving through the water.

About the Author

Terry Sparks' Naval career started as an electronics technician repairing communications, radar, computer and satellite tracking equipment. During his 8 ½ years of active duty, Terry stood watches in navigation, radar and sonar aboard diesel and missile submarines.

After leaving active duty Terry went back to school and attained a Bachelor of Science degree in Electrical Engineering.

At the 14 year point of his Navy Reserve career, he was promoted to Ensign and ultimately retired as Commander. Terry remains a member of the Navy and Marine Corps Military Auxiliary Radio System (MARS). MARS provides a backup system to military and emergency Communications.

US Federal Communications Commission Licenses: General Class Radio Telephone with Radar endorsement License; Global Maritime Distress and Safety System Maintainer License; Amateur Extra Ham License; Ships Station License; and Marine Radio Operator Permit.

Call Signs: WDA5497, AD7XL, and NNN0AYM.

Civilian positions have included Chief Engineer at a television station, Instructor at Columbia Basin College, systems engineer, and design and software development and engineering management.

Terry also retired from ABB Inc. (one of the world's largest Electrical Engineering companies) in 2008 and is now sailing somewhere in Mexico.

Table of Contents

Chapter 1 – Radar Myths

Source of Myths

It appears that most people shy away from things they do not understand or think something is too hard to learn.   In our travels we have found a few cruisers that say they do not need or do not use Radar.   So radar operation may be one of those things that some people shy away from.

For the beginner user, it may seem intimidating to consider dots on a display that may represent another vessel or even navigation aids. As a result, some cruisers simply leave the radar off or never install radar and fly by the seat of their pants hoping everyone else has radar and will not hit them. When the non-radar users make it home from a voyage alive, they create myths about not needing radar at sea.

Unfortunately, these myths tend to be heard by people preparing to cruise and occasionally lead to new cruisers not spending the money on a critical cruising tool, radar.

The next section will discuss some of the well-known myths and why they are myths.   Bottom line for radar is they are myths and you should not go to sea without radar on your boat.

The Myths

Radar is not necessary

After many years at sea on naval vessels and sailboats, I always take a strong stand the myth creators. All commercial and military vessels are required to have at least one radar on board per US Coast Guard rules. This is not intended to enhance the radar vendor's profits, but to enhance safety at sea. Safety at sea is clearly applicable to Cruisers as well as commercial vessels. It is every captain's responsibility to keep the boat ad crew safe and that means you need and must know how to operate radar.

At night at sea it is very dark with no moon. Your own navigation lights can hinder your night vision and driving your boat through the night without radar is like walking through a park with a blindfold on.

Radar requirements have even been enhanced with the implementation of the Global Maritime Distress Safety System (GMDSS) established by the International Maritime Organization (IMO)

Example
This brings to mind one of my assignments while serving in the Navy. I was asked to develop a design change for the Trident class Submarines.

The Trident submarines were developed using many new standards in the submarine industry, but also a few standards that have existed since World War II, like radar. The submarines were all built with only one radar on board.

The Trident Submarines are the largest submarines ever built by the United States. To the Navy's surprise the new Trident submarines did not meet the Coast Guard rules which required two radars for a vessel of ~16,500 surface tons. So the Navy had to retrofit a second radar and I was fortunate enough to have the task of putting the design change documentation together for Naval Sea Systems.

If the Coast Guard requires radar on almost every vessel and two radars on larger vessels, cruisers should consider why commercial vessels and the Navy comply without any complaints. On commercial and naval vessels this is also a dedicated watch station.

Knowing how to use your radar will significantly decrease the intimidation a radar display might convey to a new cruiser. If you are just starting the cruising life, keep an open mind and learn how to use your radar.

A few times you might be happy you learned how to use your radar so you are ready:

1. When you are coming into a fogged in bay or harbor.
2. When fog roles in at sea, especially at night.
3. When you are trying to enter an un-lit or super brightly lit harbor for the first time.
4. When you have a big vessel coming at you and they are not answering your radio calls.
5. To obtain navigation positions if your GPS is not functioning.
6. To get into a harbor where your charts are way off, like Mexico.
7. To identify a squall coming your way.
8. To figure out how to get around the squall.

Example
One personal example of how radar can be extremely useful was a few years ago while I was bringing a boat to Ensenada from San Jose Del Cobo.

It was approximately 10:00 PM when a cruise ship, also traveling north, lit up the ocean. Her track was to my starboard approximately a mile away, as determined from our radar. At night it can be very difficult to tell how far away a vessel of that size is especially with all the lights shining. The radar made it clear that we were safe.

Approximately a half hour later, the horizon at my stern lit up as a second cruise ship came within view. The new vessel was approximately eight miles away and appeared as though it would also go to starboard. However, with all the white lights it was very difficult to see the green and/or red bow lights.

Within a few minutes, I found the vessel had a zero bearing rate on the radar. (That means we will meet at some point we would collide and I would lose based on tonnage.) While I had the right of way, it was not clear the right of way was going to be yielded.

I called the cruise ship on channel 16 then again on 13. No answer! I tried again and again with no answer. The massive lights of the cruise ship in the total darkness of the night killed my night vision and I could not see the bow lights to determine where the ship was headed. However, the cruise ship seemed to continue have a starboard shift visually and a zero bearing rate on my radar.

Waiting a few more minutes it was clear **on my radar** that she was coming directly up my stern with a continued zero bearing rate. I came left 90 degrees and continued to hail the cruise ship.

The cruise ship officer of the deck finally answered on VHF when I was out of his way. Based on my radar information, he passed over my original tack. I was not happy as again I had the right of way, but he was bigger so he won. I believe that his not answering was his special way of motivating me to take the action.   The radar allowed me to make the right choice and take the proper action.

In 2013 my wife and were heading for Puerto Vallarta from Mazatlán Mexico.   In the middle of the night me wife called me to the cockpit. She was concerned about a land mass in front of us with a narrow passage in the middle, slightly off our course.   Since we both really knew there could not be a land mass that moved in since our last trip, I knew it had to be a squall. It was and it poured for hours. With the radar we were able prepare for the rain and to drive through the weakest spot of the squall.

I personally consider radar a necessary tool when at sea.   Granted I may only use my radar 10-20% of the time cruising, but I am clearly not in a learning mode when I turn my radar on.

I have GPS and do not need radar

GPS can pinpoint your location on earth by identifying your latitude and longitude. A chart plotter will increase the benefit of knowing your latitude and longitude by plotting your position on an electronic chart.   When your vessel is tracking along the electronic charts, it is easy to think you are safe.   You should not forget that the GPS/chart plotter display is utterly blind to your actual surroundings.

GPS cannot see nearby boats, hazards floating in the water, squalls, or through the fog to help with a port entry hazards.   Your GPS is also based on electronic charts.   They can be wrong!

Example
GPS can also be very misleading when the charts are not accurate. When sailing in US waters we get used to very good charts.   After sailing in Mexico for a few years, we found the charts are typically

wrong for most locations. We frequently drive the boat over land on the GPS and would easily miss a harbor without radar at night.

The newer digital radars provide the unique ability to overlay the radar signal over the GPS charts and also colors that define the strength of the returned signal. Being able to relate the chart to an actual coast line and harbors with radar can make cruising even safer, if the charts are accurate.

I am traveling with a group and they will help me

This myth is the best of all myths and makes me laugh every time I hear it. This is actually the stupid myth. As captain of your vessel it is up to you to get you and your crew safely back to port.

If there is bad weather, heavy fog, or a difficult port entry, the captains of other vessels, with radar, will be taking care of their vessel and crew, not you. They may help you as a friend, but the primary job they have is their own vessel's safety.

In the case of severe weather or fog, the chance of the other Captain taking care of you should be planned as non-existent.

Example

Approximately 23 years ago there were several cruisers that headed from the Northeast to Bermuda. A couple of the captains and crew of the boats in the group were clearly not qualified to make the trip. They were going only because they knew the other captains and crews were very qualified. They decided they would help them if they got in trouble.

Some heavy weather occurred and the inexperienced people decided their boat might sink. The captains of the other boats were too busy saving their vessel to help them.   Ultimately, they got scared their boats would sink and got into either their dinghies or just over the side in life vests.   The experienced crews survived and the inexperienced crews' boats came aground on the east coast.   The captain and crews of the inexperienced vessels perished.

Never forget the Bottom line at Sea.   At sea the captain of the vessel is in charge and responsible for the safety of the vessel and the crew. Should you be fortunate enough to get help from another vessel or even the Coast Guard, consider yourself a LUCK PERSON!   .

Automated Information System (AIS) took the place of Radar.

The myth that Automated Information System (AIS) is a substitute for Radar is also wrong.   AIS provides great information about ships that have AIS and are transmitting an AIS signal.   However only using AIS there is:

1. Nothing displayed for vessels without AIS transmitters.
2. Nothing is displayed for loose buoys.
3. No information displayed for a squall moving into your location.
4. An assumption by an AIS receiver that the information being received is always correct.
5. Missing needed navigation data from an AIS display. While AIS displays the Closest Point of Approach (CPA) distance and time, it does not display CPA bearing.

AIS can provide a false sense of security about other vessels just as GPS can provide a false sense of security about charted land if taken as gospel.

Do not misunderstand; I think all cruisers should have at least an AIS receiver on board connected to a chart plotter. AIS is a great tool and further enhances safety at sea, but it is <u>not a substitute for radar</u>.

<u>It is not foggy in my area so I do not need radar</u>

While cruising to new places, those new places may have fog or at least thick haze that impairs your visibility. However, Cruisers always have the blackness of the night that makes it difficult to determine where you are and where you are going.

I have been in fog so thick you could not see the bow navigation light. It is not something I planned for, but when you are transiting from one location to another, you can get into situations where you cannot see without radar.

<u>Radar is too hard to operate</u>

Radar is very easy to use, but like most things including cruising it requires a little practice to become proficient enough to make sure your radar is a useful tool. The time to learn how to use your radar is before you head out cruising. Not when you have a situation that requires the power of radar to keep you and your crew safe.

The good news is you bought this book so I am hopeful you are already motivated to learn how to use your radar. I am especially hopeful if we come head to head in the middle of a foggy night that that this book and your practice will get us through the night.

Comments

Practicing tracking contacts and getting fixes on your radar can be more important than knowing how to sail. The time to practice is first in port then at sea during the daytime when you can see what is out there and can relate the scope to what you see. On a bright sunny day with other vessels around, pick them out on your radar. They will look the same on your radar at night.

Keep in mind that radar may be used for vessel/contact avoidance and navigation when within range of land. Radar can also provide early warning for squalls.

The main purpose of this book is to help you get the most out of your radar so you are ready to cruise safely.

A few years ago I did a presentation on radar operation in Puerto Escondido Mexico. Later I received an email from one of the persons that attended my seminar.

He told me that his wife had called him to the helm every time she saw something on the radar. As you might expect his overnight passages were tough as he typically got little sleep. However she was not comfortable when any vessel was displayed on her radar display.

He said after the radar seminar they made an overnight passage. He came up on watch and found his wife was managing three contacts and was very comfortable driving their boat through the traffic as she had determined there was no threat on her own.

The seminars I do on radar include the information found in this book and on my web site. There is also a link on my web site to the article the above individual wrote as an advocate of staying safe with radar.

http://www.made-simplefor-cruisers.com/radar

Chapter 2 –Radar Basics

History

Radar is actually an acronym: RAdio Detection and Ranging (Radar) Radar was developed and in use since WWII. Radar is similar to sonar, but uses a very high frequency. Your fathometer is a type of sonar and transmits and receives audio frequencies, around 200 to 600 Hz, through the water. Radar operates at a much higher frequency, ~ 9,400,000 Hz (9.4 GHz), through the air.

Sounds travel in the air at approximately 340 meters per second (767 miles per hour) and it is about 4.3 times as fast in water as in the air or approximately 3300 miles per hour. Radio frequency waves however are electromagnetic waves and travel through the air at approximately the speed of light or 162,000 nm/Second or 300,000,000 Meters/Second.

Radar sends out a burst of energy and part of that energy will bounce back (reflected) from objects in the transmitted path. This is similar to sonar or even yelling into a canyon with audio waves, but at a much higher frequency. The time it takes for a signal to arrive at an object plus the same time for the reflected signal to get back to the source of the audio is the basic principal of both sonar and radar. Knowing the speed audio or radio frequency through the medium will allow the device to calculate the distance.

Note: If your fathometer was sitting on the hard and operated in the air and the distance to the ground was 6 feet it should read approximately 26 feet because the speed of the signal would be 4.3 time slower. However the transducer is depending on water so it will probably not read anything.

Radar was developed just before World War II. It was being tested on December 7, 1941 when the Japanese bombed Pearl Harbor. The radar then required 2 operators, one operator to turn the antenna and one operator to read the display. The radar operators actually saw the Japanese airplanes arriving, but no one had faith in the system at the time. Unfortunately, the assumption was that the radar echoes that were received were signals from US planes arriving or maybe just bad signals from a new techy device.

Radar has progressed significantly and is much simpler to use than the radar being used in 1941. Radar was once too expensive for pleasure craft use and as a result used primarily by the military at the beginning. Radar is now common used by all commercial and military vessels. Radar is also a typical installation for the majority or one might also say the smart cruisers.

Radio Wave Travel

Today cruisers use many transmitting devices aboard their boats. Each device has a specific purpose. Each device transmits radio frequency signal with a propagation that is dependent on the frequency of the radio signal being transmitted.

High Frequency (HF) signals are the lowest radio wave frequencies used on board cruising vessels. HF is used for Marine Single Side Band (SSB) and Amateur SSB radio transmissions. HF radios transmit a direct wave, a ground wave and also a sky wave.

The direct wave goes to what your antenna can see, vessels in visual sight. The ground wave is transmitted along the surface of the earth for a relatively short distance. The sky wave bounces off the ionosphere and back to the earth then back to the ionosphere, etc. When conditions are right, the sky wave may bounce back and forth all the way around the world.

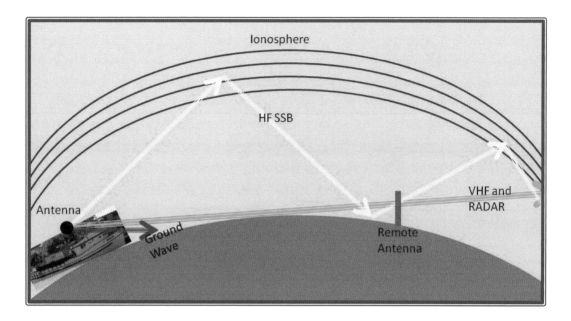

Very High Frequency (VHF) is a much higher frequency than HF and tends to transmit line of sight. That means the transmitting and receiving antennas must basically be able to see each other to communicate. As a result antenna height is the most important aspect for longest range VHF radio communications.

Cruisers use VHF for Marine VHF radio and some Amateur radio. When a VHF radio wave gets beyond the horizon it continues out into space and typically does not return.

Radar is probably the highest frequency radio wave on board a typical cruising vessel. Radar is line of site and will send a signal out to past the horizon and then into space. There will be a very small amount of bending of the signal over the horizon, but for normal operation signals beyond the horizon should be considered weather related. So the good news is that when the signal goes past the horizon, it can provide valuable information about a weather front or maybe a squall heading to your way.

For more information on VHF and HF communications, consider either or both of my books: "Communications Made Simple for Cruisers" or "A New Ham I Am * Made Simple for Cruisers".

The Horizon

Since our earth is approximately round, very high frequency radio waves and light keep going into space beyond the horizon. As a cruiser, it is important that you know approximately where the horizon is so you can use your transmitting equipment and understand what the actual distance of your vision is at sea.

For example: If you see a vessel coming up on the horizon, how far is the vessel from your vessel? That is approximately the same distance for a radars distance except a radar is usually a bit higher that your location in the cockpit. Distance is proportional to height.

The horizon in nautical miles is equal to 1.17 times the square root of the sum of heights of the object looking and being looked at.

$$NM = 1.17\sqrt{H1 + H2}$$

Where: NM = Nautical Miles, H1 = Height of looking person or radar, H2 = Height of thing being looked at.

Since this is not going to be a math course, here are some examples of various heights.

Height of self	Height of object being looked at	Horizon
8 foot visual	8 foot object	4.68 NM
25 foot Antenna	0 feet at horizon	5.85 NM
25 foot Antenna	25 foot vessel	8.27 NM
25 foot Antenna	50 foot vessel on the horizon	10.0 NM
50 foot Antenna	50 foot Structure	11.7 NM
50 foot Antenna	1000 foot Squall	37.9 NM

These distances are probably not the distance you may have imagined as they are very close based on many observations you may have had on land at various elevations. Remember everything at sea is at sea level….

The Basics

Radar transmits a directional signal, then goes into a listening mode for a predetermined time. The radar is listening for returned signals (echoes) of the transmitted radio frequency energy. The transmitted energy will bounce off objects and then return to the transmitting antenna. This transmit receive sequence occurs very quickly and the returned echoes return before the antenna has physically rotated minutely from the direction where the energy was transmitted.

So a radar transmits, goes to the receive mode for a period, then transmits again while the antenna is rotated 360 degrees relatively very slow as compared to the speed the transmitted signal is moving.

Again, radar echoes are similar to audio echoes. E.g. Yelling into a canyon and hearing your voice bounce back later. Radar just uses a higher frequency and measures the time between transmit and reception of the signal. It is that simple

While the principal of an echo returning to its origin is very simple, the echo is only valuable when we can display the echoes in a meaningful way on a display.

How the Display Works

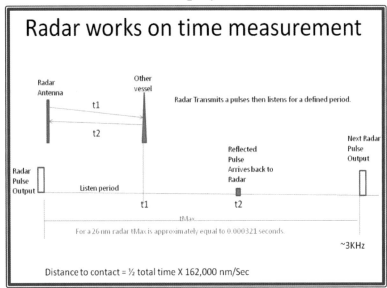

Radar works on time measurement

Radar Antenna

Other vessel

t1

t2

Radar Transmits a pulses then listens for a defined period.

Radar Pulse Output

Listen period

Reflected Pulse Arrives back to Radar

Next Radar Pulse Output

t1

t2

tMax

For a 26 nm radar tMax is approximately equal to 0.000321 seconds.

~3KHz

Distance to contact = ½ total time X 162,000 nm/Sec

The display starts drawing a picture from the center of the display to the outer edge of the display as it waits for returned echoes. Since the radar signal must go to the target and return to the antenna, the time it takes for the signal to travel both ways is twice the time it takes to get to the target.

To display the returned, echo, signal at the proper location, the display basically scans outward from the center of the display (where you are) in the same direction as the signal was transmitted at ½ the speed the signal being transmitted to the other vessel or land target was transmitted.

The display starts the sweep outward with the transmitted pulse and extends only to the outer ring of the display. However the transmitted signal will continue on and the transmitter will not transmit until a specified time period. The time period is typically selectable on most radars as to using long pulses of short pulses.

In other words, if a signal were to take 1 second to get to an object at the maximum range of the selected display range, the return signal would arrive and be plotted in 2 seconds.

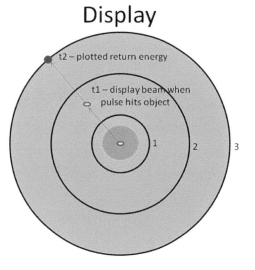

As discussed before radar and display operate much quicker than seconds as the transmitted signal is moving at approximately the speed of light, 300,000,000 meters/S and the display is slower at 150,000,000 meters/S.
If you are on the three mile range, the transmitted signal will go out to an object 3 miles from the radar,

hit the object and the reflected signal will return to the antenna. The display trace will be at the three mile point when the return signal arrives. The trace will create a mark at the three mile point proportional to the amount of energy that was received from the object.

What the returned echo will look like on the display will be an elongated, round, bright or dim mark. The mark on the display will not look like a ship or any other object that may reflect the energy. Land however does provide useful shape information such as points of land to be discussed more in detail later in this book.

The transmitted signal does not stop just because the display got to the outer ring of the display, but will continue on into space. Any additional echoes are not displayed as the receiver is no longer listening. The radar then gets ready for a new transmitted pulse of energy as the antenna is rotated slightly. The slight antenna rotation is relative to the frequency of the transmit/receive cycle time.

The transmit/receive cycle time is the repeating process that will be based on selection of long or short pulses via the radar's menu. Technically the setting is changing the Pulse Repetition Rate (PRF). A higher PRF has a shorter pulse that is being transmitted and will listen for a shorter time than the long PRF setting. A short PRF will result in better definition of a targets reflected signal as the shorter pulse will result in more reflected pulses were the long pules may return one big pulse for an entire object.

The returned signal is proportional to reflectivity of the target and not always proportional to the size of the target. E.g. Metal boats will reflect significantly more than fiberglass or wood boats.

Don't forget to install a radar reflector on your boat if it is constructed of wood or fiberglass so you can be seen by other vessels radars.

Relative Bearing

Cruising radar displays are typically set up to display relative to your bow direction for targets.

That means that contacts displayed at 000 degrees on your radar are coming from beyond the bow of your boat. The radar's right side is starboard (090), the left side is port (270), and the bottom of the display is what is behind the stern of the boat (180). In other words if you see a contact on the display's left side, look left and you might be able to see the actual contact.

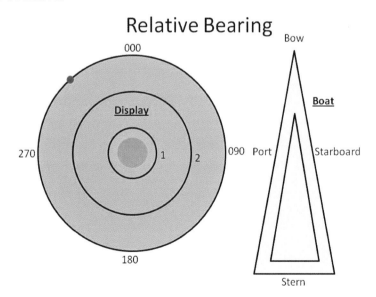

Some radar installations may have a heading reference available so that the top of the display may be selected as true north. When true bearing is used, contacts on the port side may appear any place on your display as the top of the display would always be true or magnetic north.

There is an advantage for the operator when a heading reference sets the top of the display to north. With a heading reference, as your vessel changes heading, the contact(s) are always displayed in the same location on the radar's display.

Without the heading reference an object tends to move around with your boats movement. Basically for relative bearing if your boat was to turn 90 degrees, the object will move 90 degrees in the opposite direction on your display. With an external reference providing true bearing the object would remain in the same location on your display.

Most large commercial vessels use true bearing. They also go to sea with dedicated, highly skilled radar operator.

Most cruisers tend to single hand, especially at night. Most cruisers are not skilled radar operators. As a result the recommended approach for radar operation on a cruising boat is relative bearing mode. Relative bearing keeps it simple as a contact displayed on the left side of the display will be on the left side of the boat. Using north up can make radar analysis more difficult and confusing for a shorthanded crew given the other things we have to do on watch in the dark of night.

In relative bearing, if I see a vessel that has a CPA that will be in front of me on the radar, I know I have to do something.

Chapter 3 – Expectations for Radar

Understanding what you see

A realistic expectation of what you will be able to see on a radar display is important for a cruiser to understand.

Sometimes radar sales people can lead you to believe that you want the longest distance radar because it is so much better and you will pick up contacts earlier. The reality is that the radar can only pick up what it can see and that is always just slightly more than the distance to the horizon.

The longer range radars may have a higher power output, a more sensitive receiver, but in actuality the main difference is how long the radar listens before it transmits again. When longer range radar sends out a pulse, the next pulse will not occur for a longer period than shorter range radars. Since a longer range takes more time for the reflected signal to return, the radar will listen longer on the highest range. On the shorter ranges, radar only listens for the displayed time.

Remember, the radar signal leaves the earth at just past the horizon, longer range radar may see clouds 36 miles out instead of 24 miles, but not other vessels.

What can I see on Radar?

<u>Prospective</u>
- The top of the Radar is normally the direction of the bow of the boat.
- Things <u>close</u> to each other tend to <u>combine</u> into one object. If you saw the movie "Top Gun" they had to change angles to the approaching airplanes to determine there was more than one. The same effect is true on a boat.

<u>Distance</u>
- Approximately out to the horizon for other vessels.
- Beyond the horizon:
  - Tall ships peeking over the horizon.
  - Land beyond the horizon if it is high enough.
  - Towers along the shore line.
  - Weather fronts and squalls can be seen beyond the horizon.
- Sea return (The radio waves bouncing off the ocean and back to the radar. Sea Return will be the strongest close to your vessel.)

<u>Other vessels</u>
- Other vessels less than approximately 10 NM away.
- Display may appear as fuzzy for the appearance of contacts if return is not strong.
- Contacts may <u>appear</u> and <u>disappear</u> with the waves shifting yours vessel and the other vessel(s) up and down.
  - Changing the height of either vessel changes the distance to the horizon.
  - Waves may actually cover the other vessel so there is no vessel displayed.

Land

- Land can be farther than the 10 NM with mountains. The distance is dependent on the elevation of the land.
- Points of land can be very distinctive.
- Mountains may be just one big bright spot.

Navigation Aids

- Navigation Aids may look like vessels, but do not move.

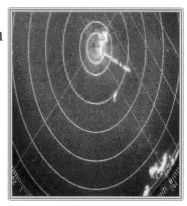

  - The movement of a navigation aid will be the same as your vessel. E.g. closing or opening the distance at your speed and direction.
- Some Navigation aids such as RACON (frequently used for traffic lane separation) send a signal back when scanned by a radar signal. They identify the buoy using Morse code dots and dashes that will be displayed on your radar's display.
- When a Search and Rescue Transponders (SART) is scanned it will send back 12 dots in a line similar to the dashes of the traffic lane markers above. The dot closest to you is the location of the SART

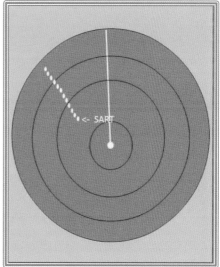

Chapter 4 – It's All About Motion

Evaluating Motion

First let's look at a couple of cockpit calculations that can come in handy in the cockpit visually or with your radar.   Both the 3 minute and 6 minute rule are easy and typically will eliminate the need for a calculator to obtain a rough speed or better yet how long will it take another vessel to arrive at your vessel.

The Three Minute Rule
The Three (3) minute rule states that you can add two zeroes (multiply by 100) to a vessel's speed or combined speeds and the resultant number will be the distance that vessel(s) will travel, in yards, in three minutes. So if a vessel is traveling at 10 knots, it will travel 1000 yards in three minutes and one nautical mile in six minutes.

Case 1: We are traveling at 5 nm/hr
Solution: So 5 +00
                                   = 500 yards/3 minutes
                                   Since 2000 yards = <u>1nm,</u>
                                   And then 2000/500
                                   = <u>4 periods of 3 minutes for 1nm</u>
                   So Then: 4 periods x 3 minutes = **<u>12 minutes/nm</u>**

Case 2: Our vessel is traveling at 5 knots with other vessel coming head on at 15 knots 6 miles away!
Solution: Adding the two vessels 5+15 = 20 nm/Hr
                                   So 20 +00
                                   Combined = 2000 yards in 3 minutes
                                   = <u>1nm in 3 minutes</u>
So we will meet the other vessel in:
                                   3minutes x 6 nm = **<u>18 minutes till we meet</u>**

The Six Minute Rule

The six minute rule states that you can divide the speed in knots by ten and that will be the distance traveled in 6 minutes.

Case 1: We are Traveling at 10 nm/hr

Solution: So Then: 10/10 = **1 nm**

We will travel 1 nm in 6 Minutes

Case 2: Own ship 5 knots with other vessel coming head on at 15 knots 10 miles away!

Solution: So: 5+15 = 20 nm

And: 20/10 = 2 nm in a 6 minute period.

We will meet the other vessel in:

10 miles / 2nm per period = 5 Periods

So Then: 5 Periods * 6 Minutes = 30 Minutes

Relative Bearing

Relative bearing is typically used for radar displays on cruising boats. So we will touch on relative bearing again in this section on relative motion.

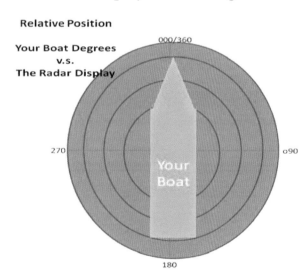

Relative bearing means that the bearing of the display is the same as the bearings for your boat. That is the top of the display representing 000 degrees is the bow and the bottom of the display representing 180 degrees is the stern of your boat.

Some integrated GPS and radar installations may provide the option for North up. Either true north or magnetic north as selected is display at the top of the display.   For a north up GPS display, if the radar display is overlaid onto the GPS display the radar will probably be in a north mode also.   When side by side GPS and Radar are displayed, the radar is probably in relative bearing.

For Consideration: I prefer using my GPS chart display in relative bearing also. That mode is referred to as course up or heading up on some GPS chart plotters.   Course up provides a better sense of what is ahead on the GPS similar to the radar.   Like with the radar in relative bearing, I never have to figure out what I am looking at when I compare the GPS, radar, or the real world around me.   I also stay in Magnetic bearing so the compass also agrees with where I am going. This is a big change from my Navy days where everything was true north up, but our radar team was 3 people and there were many more driving the boat as a separate task.

Bearing Rate
Bearing rate is a term that refers to the change in bearing of a contact per unit of time.   e.g. A contact changed 10 degrees in one minute provides a 10 degree per minute bearing change.

If a contact is changing 10 degrees every minute it has a rapid bearing rate and depending on the range of the contact should not collide with your vessel.

If a contact is not changing bearing it is referred to as a zero bearing rate contact. A **Zero bearing rate is considered a collision course**.

Evaluating a Contacts Motion

Movement Based on Shore Located Radar

To provide a prospective as to what a vessel will look like on a radar display, we need to first consider basic movement of a single vessel and a fixed radar site.

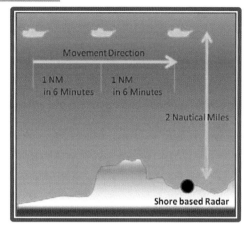

Using a shore based radar and a single vessel traveling at sea we keep the relative movement at a minimum. If a vessel is north of our radar location traveling on a course of 090 (from West to the East) the vessel will move across the ocean from our left toward our right in a straight line.   It will appear the same on radar.

Example

To keep the example simple, we will use the example of a vessel traveling at 10 Knots on a heading of 090 degrees.   The shore based radar shall be set exactly two nautical miles south of the vessels West to East track.

From the 3 minute rule we know that the boat will travel 1000 yards in three minutes and one nautical mile every six minutes.

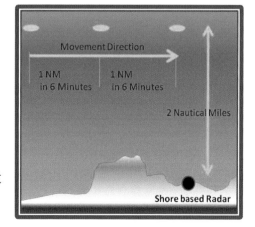

On a radar display, the reflected dots will be displayed from the contact and will move continuously across the display from the left to the right side of the display. The contact will be at the closest point to us when it is perpendicular (at 90 degrees) to us or due north in this case.

If we mark two or three points on the display, it will be easy to identify the vessel is in fact on a course of 090. (Un-like the graphics used here, the dots will disappear so they need to be marked by some method, discussed later, to determine the direction.)

Motion Including Our Boat

Now we will place the radar platform on a second vessel, our boat.

Our boat will be moving due north (getting closer to the track of the other vessel) at ten knots.

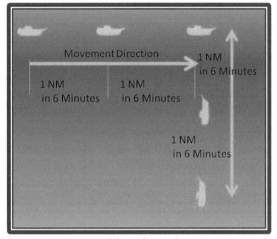

Since we are traveling at the same speed and we are the same distance apart, our vessel will be approaching the exact same location as the vessel on the 090 course.

Again, each vessel is traveling at the same speed having the same distance toward the same point. As you might have already expected, they are headed for a collision if no one does changes course or speed.

The dots on a radar display will show relative motion. That is the sum of our motion with that of the motion of the other vessel. For each sweep of the radar it will show the other vessel getting closer to our boat.

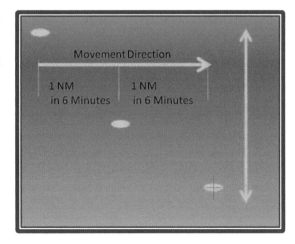

Since both vessels are moving at the <u>same speed</u> <u>90 degrees apart,</u> there will be a constant bearing (45 degrees to port) of the approaching vessel.

We can now start to see how relative motion works between the two vessels. <u>It is important to recognize that the other vessel is viewed on our display as moving closer to our vessel on the reciprocal angle (45 degrees to starboard).</u>

That is what is really happening, we are on a collision course any time we have a constant bearing on another vessel's approach. (Zero Bearing Rate)

Our display would show a resultant plot for the vessel on a constant bearing of 315 degrees.

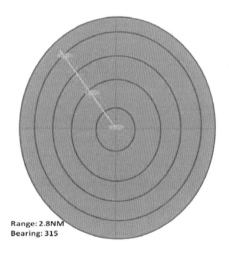

Range: 2.8NM
Bearing: 315

For those of you that have a trigonometry background, it is easy to see that the resultant angle is 45 degrees. When we have a 45 degree angle off our bow, we subtract 45 degrees from the 000 or 360 degrees to obtain a direction from our vessel with respect to our vessel of a bearing of 315. (The other vessel would see us coming at 045 degrees if they had their radar on.)

Don't get discouraged, you do not need to know trig to operate a radar. The radar display will read out at the 315 degrees when you place the cursor over the contact.

In this example, if someone does not turn or change speed, we will have a collision at sea.

BEWARE OF ZERO BEARING RATES!

<u>**An Evasive Movement**</u>
When we determine that we have a zero bearing rate we need to do something quick and significantly so the other vessel is aware of our change.

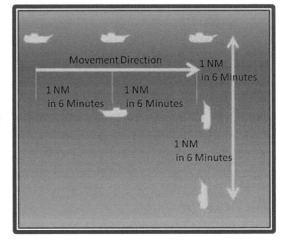

In most cases you can speed up, slow down, turn left, or turn right. (If the vessels are coming head to head, The rules indicate you should make a significant turn to starboard.)

(For this example we will wait until the first six minutes period has passed, to keep the math simple, and then we will turn our vessel.)

After the first six minutes, we see we are on a collision course and turn to the left 90 degrees as the other vessel is headed east. The 90 degree turn will result in our vessel now traveling due west or at 270 degrees. If both

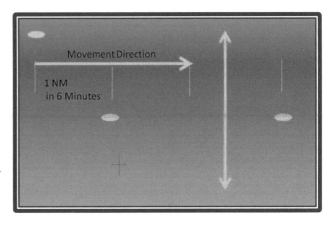

vessels were to make a small change, you could still end up with a zero bearing rate.)

Our new heading is now opposite that of the other vessel's heading at 090 degrees. Since both vessels are traveling at 10 knots, going in opposite directions this will result in a separation speed of 20 knot.

Using the 3 minute rule, 20 knots is 2000 yards of separation (one nautical mile) in 3 minutes.

During the six minute period, the two vessels will separate by two nautical miles, west to east and maintain an approximate one mile, north to south separation.

In 3 minutes you could have head north again and you will fall behind the other vessel by approximately one mile as a CPA.

Example on Our Radar Display

The radar display will present the above contact information in approximately the same way as the pictures above. The main difference is that there will be a moving dot instead of a string of dots. In order to keep track of the relative motion, you must mark the vessels travel with the cursor, EBL and VRM, or maybe even a grease pencil.

Our first mark would be from the contacts origination (seeing the other vessel). The second mark would be after the first six minute period.

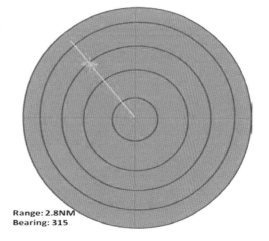

Note: Placing the bearing line over the original contacts point would allow us to see rapidly that the contact is walking down the bearing line or in other words the contact has a zero bearing rate.

Range: 2.8NM
Bearing: 315

This can be very useful as it provides for more time to decide what to do.

Initial Contact:

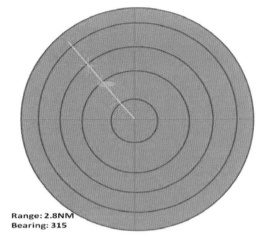

Range: 2.8NM
Bearing: 315

Six Minutes Later:

After change of course and Six more minutes:

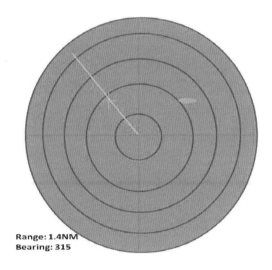

Range: 1.4NM
Bearing: 315

Departing Position:

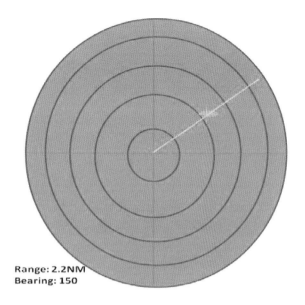

Range: 2.2NM
Bearing: 150

The contact will actually appear many times between the original position and the final position as the radar antenna rotates and presents the latest position of the returned signal of our contact.

If you were to use a grease pencil, like we did in the Navy, you could put a dot every so often and the dots would actually form a rough line.

Understanding how your vessel is causing part of the movement on the display (relative motion) is important.

- If the bearing rate is changing fast, you should be OK.
- If the bearing rate is the same or changing very slowly, you should be concerned.
- If another vessel changes course, you need to re-evaluate so forget the prior points.

If all of this is still confusing, read through it again.

If you still need help, send me a note at p-t_on_sunyside@live.com and I will be happy to help as the concept of relative motion is important to be able to understand what you seeing on a radar display.

If the Bering rate is big the CPA will also be big!

Chapter 5 – Controls and Functions

Basic Display

Basics

Typically cruising radar transmits and receives approximately 3000 times per second as the radar rotates the 360 degrees around your boat at approximately 40 rpm. That is clearly much faster than any cruiser can look around their vessel for other ships or obstacles. 3,000 times per second is equal to 4,320,000 pulses per minute. That means your radar will check every degree approximately forty times per minute.

To see a contact on your display, the radar's controls must be set correctly. While this is not difficult it is often the reason people have issues with radar operation. In this section we will discuss how to make sure you see what the radar is finding around your boat.

Clearly, the larger a contact is on the display, the easier it is to identify and track. The size of a contact is dependent on the amount of reflected energy, but can also be changed by the following control settings.

- Range setting
- Gain setting
- Trail on/off
- Anti Sea
- Rain settings
- Brightness
- Contrast /Tone

The physical parameters of an object will vary the size of the object on the display. The primary factors that impact the displayed object size include the type of material; size of the object; general shape of the object and the surface angel(s) of the object. As a result it is possible to have a large dot for a small vessel and a small or no dot for a large vessel.

Larger is not always better: As an example take a look at the shape of stealth Navy vessels. The designed in angles of these large vessels results in sending the reflected wave into the sky instead of back to the radar.

Unlike Navy vessels, we cruisers want to be seen. Radar reflectors actually result in more echoes going back to the radar that create a larger dot on the display.

Frequently large power boats with engines below the waterline can be difficult to see on radar when they are constructed out of fiberglass and they do not have a radar reflector.

There are also special buoys cruisers should be aware of called RACON buoys and SART buoys that transmit a signal when scanned by radar. These buoys will present a significantly larger display than the size of the buoy. The RACON buoys send Morse code to identify who they are and the SART buoys send out 12 dots to help search and rescue teams find them.

A typical basic radar display is shown below:

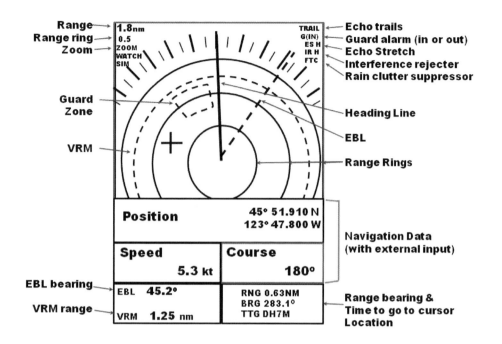

Things On the Display

Moving down the left side of the display picture above and then down the right side.

- ➢ Range – Identifies where the cursor is located from the center.
- ➢ Range ring – Identifies the spacing between range rings.
- ➢ Zoom – On function allows you to zoom in to a portion of your display around the position of the cursor.
- ➢ Guard Zone – Allows the operator to set up an area of interest where and alarm will sound if a contact is detected

in this area. This function can result in false alarms as sea return can also result in alarms.

- VRM – is the variable range mark as displayed typically with a dashed circle that may be increased or decreased in size.
- EBL bearing – Digital readout of the position of the Electronic Bearing Line.
- VRM range – The VRM Range is a digital readout of the distance from the center of the circle to the dashed VRM circle.
- Echo trails – Tells the operator if trailing is turned on or off. Trail allows a returned signal from a prior sweep to remain on the display to provide a sense of movement for a contact. Set to long trails for the best results.
- Guard alarm (in or out) – Tells the operator if the Guard range is on or off. E.g. whether the guard area will sound an alarm or not.
- Echo Stretch – Tells the operator that Echo Stretch is enabled. Echo Stretch increases the size of a small return signal to make it easier to see. It also increases sea return and rain drops so it is not the ultimate aid to identify a contact.
- Interference rejecter – Tells the operator that the interference rejection is on. The Interference rejecter is supposed to help reject other frequencies that may be interfering with your radar. (Never used it)

- Rain clutter suppressor – Tells the operator that FTC, rain clutter rejection is on. We will discuss later, but this function can reduce the gain of your receiver and result in missed contacts when adjusted wrong.
- Heading Line – The heading line is displayed when the operator is using the true bearing mode. Since in true bearing the top of the display will be north, the Heading Line will point out to the operator which way the boat is traveling on the display.
- EBL – The Electronic Bearing Line works in conjunction with the VMR to identify a point on the display. It can also be used to track a contact to assure the bearing rate is greater than zero.
- Range Rings – the Range rings provide a quick estimate of how far out from your vessel contacts and/or land masses are located. This display shows 0.5 miles per ring so the outer ring would be 1.5 miles.
- Navigation Data – Navigation data is only displayed when input into the radar display from an external source.
- Range bearing & Time to go to cursor Location – The range to a waypoint may also displayed when input from an external source.

Initial Settings for Your Radar

Basic controls and settings for "most" simple radars include:

Be Careful: Some of the controls impact the sensitivity of the received signal and/or change the display so that it is difficult to see contacts.

- ➢ **Tuning** – Adjustment of receiver frequency to the transmitted frequency. This control actually tunes the receiver so it can hear the transmitted signal that is returned. **Leave this control in automatic unless you see no returns with the gain control at the highest level.**

- ➢ **Gain** – Sensitivity of receiver is set to the highest possible without blanking out the display with sea return. **If available, leave in automatic gain. If manual is selected, go to the highest range on the display and increase the gain until the display shows sea return over most of the display. Slowly decrease the gain until you see occasional sea return all over the display.**

- ➢ **STC** – Suppressing Sea Clutter is used to reduce sea return clutter near your vessel. Be careful though as it is reducing the return signal gain near your vessel and you could miss other vessels or buoys. **I leave mine OFF as I may miss other objects if not adjusted perfectly.**

- ➢ **A/C Rain** – Cuts down on the signals returned by rain. Again, be careful as it is reducing the gain of your radar's receiver. **I leave mine OFF as it may mask small object.**

- **FTC** – Suppresses rain clutter from heavy storms is similar to A/C Rain. . **I leave mine OFF as it may mask small object.**

- **VRM** – Variable Range Mark may be used to aid in evaluating the progress of other vessels. To track contacts and to be discussed later.

- **ELB** – Electronic Bearing Line may be used to aid in evaluating the progress of other vessels. EBL is used to track contacts bearings and to be discussed in more detail later.

- **Brill and Tone** – Back light and Contrast are similar to TV and computer display adjustments. **The best adjustment is based on your light conditions and personal preferences.**

- **Trail** – leaves the last return(s) dimmer for the next rotation to help you access another vessel's movement by making an elongated dot at the location of the other vessel. The elongation represents the relative motion of the vessel, buoy, or other target being displayed. **If your vessel is relatively stable, trail can be very useful. If your vessel is yawing a lot, trail can be misleading.**

- **Rings** – Turns range rings on and off. **I leave mine on** as it provides a quick reference as to how far from me the returned target being displayed is located.

- **Off Center** – Moves vessel to display more information. Shifts the center of the display such that you can see more aft or forward of your vessel. This allows other vessel to be displayed farther away on a lower scale range. **Off for sailboats, on for higher speed power boats** to shift boat position to the stern direction on the display and provide more coverage forward of the boat on the display.

- ➤ **Range** – When **off shore primarily use the 6 or 8 nm maximum range** setting. The range should be changed frequently when visibility is poor. Remember, the <u>lower the range, the larger the target</u> will be displayed and conversely the higher the range the smaller the target will be. Large targets are always easy to see on the display. E.g. a target on the 6 NM rage will be twice the size on a 3 NM range making it easier to see. Recommended use of Range control:

  - **Try to use no range setting of more than 6 nm for extended period**

  - **Be sure and change range several times per hour to all ranges.**

    - **This will show any potential weather/squalls coming on upper ranges.**

    - **On the lower ranges, a potentially missed target or buoy will appear larger to make sure you see it.**

    - **On very low ranges you can even see very small vessels moving rapidly.**

  - **Don't forget that fiberglass and wood boats make poor reflectors. The engines are usually at or below the waterline so do not count on a good return unless the vessel has a radar reflector.**

- When near land set range low enough to see the land. So when 3 miles off shore, you may want to use the 3 mile range as base. This will also enhance your ability to see small craft coming at you from the shoreline.

- When coming into a busy harbor use ½ to 1 nm so contacts are easily detected and yet you will have adequate response time for any situations that may arrive.

Chapter 6 – Contact Avoidance

Contact Avoidance is a key use of radar. When you are in a busy harbor, this can be very challenging for one person. Radar can allow the operator to quickly assess the approximate distance and location another vessel is located and how close that other vessel will potentially come near your vessel.

Other times when you are off shore, radar can see through the night and fog to find potential hazards.

Knowing about potential hazards off shore or in harbors in advance will help you to take the proper evasive action early to avert a potentially dangerous situation

Zero Bearing Rate

A zero bearing rate contact has been discussed before, but it is a key topic for contact avoidance, the following information provides an additional look at this subject.

The term zero bearing rate is when your movement and the movement of another vessel is combined, there is a constant bearing to the contact. This can be observed visually for contacts you can see, but becomes obvious using radar when the contact is walking down the cursor line or an Electronic Bearing Line (EBL). If there is no bearing change that means that you and the other contact will meet at some point and the outcome will not be pretty.

When you have a zero bearing rate contact, you can turn right, turn left, speed up, or slow down and the bearing rate will increase to a more favorable rate of change. That also means that the contact will be farther away from you at its closest point (CPA).

It is important to remember that both <u>the contact and you are creating this zero bearing rate</u>, not just the contact. The recommended course correction should be significant, 45 to 90 degrees so the contact vessel knows you have made the change and does not make a change that may result in a zero bearing rate again. After making a change, re-check to assure the new CPA provides adequate separation between vessels.

When passing head on you should strive for a Port to Port passing, unless you have an agreement with the other vessel to do otherwise via VHF radio. If a correction is required for a head on zero bearing rate, be sure to come <u>right</u> 45 to 90 degrees

It is always a good idea to try and communicate with the other vessel(s) you see visually or on your radar. This is especially true during reduced visibility conditions so that everyone remains on the same page.

Cockpit Calculations

Cross Multiplication
If you are not familiar with cross multiplication, it is real easy and real handy when things are proportional.

If we say that the distance traveled divided by the time of travel we can also say the new distance traveled divided by the unknown time must also be true or equal.

Solving for the unknown value is then getting the unknown by itself on one side of the equation and the known values on the other side of the equation. (Actually we are multiplying or dividing both sides of the equation to move a quantity to the other side, but it looks like we just shifted across.)

EXAMPLE

So using proportions:

$$\frac{\text{Distance Contact Moved (DCM)}}{\text{Time to move above distance (TMD)}} = \frac{\text{Distance to CPA (DCPA)}}{\text{Time to CPA (TCPA)}}$$

$$\frac{(DCM)}{(TMD)} = \frac{(DCPA)}{(TCPA)}$$

Solving for TCPA becomes:

$$TCPA = \frac{DCPA * TMD}{DCM}$$

Using the data from the example

$$\frac{30NM}{1\ Hour} = \frac{35\ NM}{TCPA}$$

1 hour = 60 minutes

So by cross multiplication we get:

$$\frac{35NM * 60\ Minutes}{30\ NM} = 70\ Minutes\ to\ CPA$$

Three Minute Rule

The three minute rule may be the most important rule for a cruiser to memorize and is very simple. The rule is very helpful when you are trying to maintain contact avoidance and single handing.

Before defining the rule again, let's look at the basics of movement again.

Example 1

1. Our vessel is heading for a point at 10 knots and the distance to the point is 20 nautical miles. How long will it take to arrive at the point?

$$\frac{20NM}{10 \text{ NM/hour}} = \textbf{2 hours}$$

Example 2

2. We have 2 head on contacts, 20 nautical miles apart, each traveling at 10 knots. How long until the vessels meet?

10 knots (vessel 1) + 10 knots (vessel 2) = 20 knots closing speed.

$$\frac{20 \text{ NM}}{20 \text{ NM/hour}} = \textbf{1 hour}$$

Now with the 3 Minute Rule

The three (3) minute rule (3MR) says that a vessel traveling at any speed will travel that speed times 100 (add two zeros) in yards after 3 minutes.

Example 1 with the 3MR

1. Again our vessel is heading for a point at 10 knots and the distance to the point is 20 nautical miles. How long will it take to arrive at the point?

- The vessel traveling at 10 knots it will travel 1000 yards in 3 minutes.

- 20 nautical miles is equal to 40,000 yards. Applying the 3 minute rule, 40,000/1000 = 40 periods of 3 minutes.

- So for forty, three minute periods: 40 * 3 = 120 minutes. Or the same results from before of 2 hours. Same results easier calculation!

Example 2 with the 3MR

2. Again we have 2 head on contacts, 20 nautical miles apart, each traveling at 10 knots. How long until the vessels meet?

- The two vessels traveling at 10 knots toward each other (10 + 10 = 20) will travel one nautical mile (2000 yards) in three minutes.

- The time to travel the 20 nautical miles and meet (20 NM = 40,000 yards.) So 40,000/2,000 = 20 periods of 3

- So then 20 three minute periods or 20 * 3 = 60 minutes. OR 1 hours. Same results easier calculation!

My Boats Speed

We frequently travel at 7 knots on our boat (700 yards per three minutes). So I usually rough it out as 2000 yards in 3 periods of 3 minutes or approximately 9 minutes per nautical mile. If your boat averages approximately 5 knots then that would be 500 yards per 3 minutes or one nautical mile in 2000/500 = 4, 3 minute periods or a 12 minute mile. Makes for a good Guesstement of arrival time.

Using this rule of thumb can be very helpful, but I always keep a calculator in the cockpit to calculate CPAs and other things that come up.

Example

When will you meet a ship coming at you 1 nm away at 15 knots, if you are going 5 knots toward the contact vessel?

Answer: 15+ 5 = 20 Knots/hour Or 2000 Yards In 3 minutes. 2000 Yards is 1nm so the answer is 3 minutes.

Example

It is 12:15 and we are making 5 knots to the good through the water to a point 4 miles away. What is the latest we will be at the point 4 miles away?

Long hand solution

- 4 miles X 2000 Yards = 8000 Yards
- 5 Knots X 2000/60 = 166.67 yards per minute

- 8000 yards / 166.67 = 47.99 minutes
- 12:15 + 47.99 minutes = 1:03 PM

Cockpit hand Solution: Using the 3 Minute Rule, we know at 5 knots we will do 500 yards in 3 minutes. To travel 4 miles or 8000 yards it will take 16, 3 minute periods.

So 16 X 3 = 48 minutes
And 12:15 + 48 = 1:03 PM

Play with speed and distance calculations a bit and see how else you can apply the rules of thumb to keep from having to use a calculator in the cockpit.

Closest Point of Approach

Meaning

The closest point of approach is referred to as CPA. CPA is the bearing, range, and time of the point where another vessel will be closest to your vessel. The CPA will actually be when the contact is perpendicular to your vessel from the other vessels relative movement plot.

Knowing the CPA will provide more reaction time to potentially dangerous situations that would otherwise require quick action later. Knowing a contact's CPA early should provide you with more time to take evasive action if required.

Example

I remember one time I had a "seasoned sailor" with me and we were in a significant layer of fog. We could see approximately 100 feet ahead of the boat. My friend asked to take the helm. While at the helm he was diligently monitoring the radar and the GPS display as we cut through the fog. After a short time, I asked my friend if he needed help. I also asked if there were any contacts on the radar. He said, "No I am OK, I only have one contact and he is approximately 500 yards to port. We should be OK as he has had the same bearing for some time." At that point I yelled, hard right rudder. Within a few seconds a fishing boat came out of the fog. The boat was approximately where we would have been had we maintained course and speed.

Check CPA on all contacts as soon as possible to make sure you are on a safe course!

Finding CPA

When you identify a new contact you should mark it's location with something. I usually use the cursor, but this will be discussed more in the next section. When you get a contact, place your EBL over the contact so you can quickly detect a zero bearing rate situation. You can then run your Variable Range Marker (VRM) out to provide a crossing mark between the VRM and EBL at the present location of the contact.

When you mark the contact note the time. Keep an eye on the contact for a while to see how fast it is moving on your display. Turning on the radar's "Trailing" function can help define the contacts direction of movement. Depending on the range you are on, a given contact will move faster or slower as the display represents more or less nautical miles.

Make sure the contact is not walking down the EBL as that would indicate a zero bearing rate.

As soon as possible create a line, with say a ruler, between the cursor's position and the contact's new location on the display. Then observe where the ruler is closest to your vessel, bearing and range. Note: The CPA will be located where a line from the center of the display is perpendicular to the ruler. You can also use your cursor or your VRM to test where the contact will be closest while holding the ruler in place. Using the cursor you have to rotate it back and forth around where you believe the CPA is to identify the exact CPA point. Remember your vessel is headed to 000 degrees relative to your boat on your display.

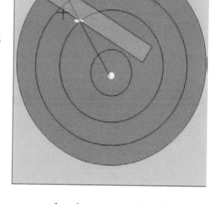

The Ace of Spades and the King of Diamonds CPA

A couple of years ago while I was preparing for a radar seminar for the Pacific Puddle Jumpers (PPJ) in Puerto Vallarta Mexico I came up with a simple way for a single handing cruiser to determine the location of CPA. Advertising for the PPJ folks to bring an Ace and King playing card to the seminar clearly enhanced the curiosity for coming to the seminar ad as a result it was well attended by over 30 people.

The concept is simple and works as follows. You can use any card that fits on your display to draw a line similar to the ruler above. While holding the card on the other vessels relative travel path, place the other card up tight against the first card and move the second card so that the other end of the card passes through the center of the display. The CPA is then where the two cards meet on the same side as the center of the display.

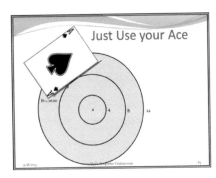

Take a look at the attached pictures to help better understand the Ace and King method.

Lay the Ace or actually any card or ruler along the relative course line of the other vessel.

Now push the King up against the ACE and through the center of the display. As indicated, the CPA is where the cards meet.

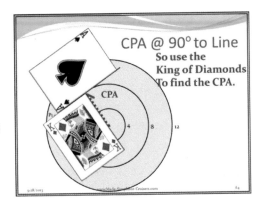

Tricks to Track a Contact

To keep track of what a contact is doing you can use the Cursor, bearing line, EBL and VRM together, and even a grease pencil. If you use a grease pencil, be sure and use a plastic cover on your display so you do not damage the display.

Since the return signal can be a big dot, when we are looking for CPA we can use the center of the dot as the reference point. We are looking for an approximate CPA only. If the contact's CPA is out 500 yards or so, we have nothing to be concerned over. But need to continue monitoring for any potential turns.

Examples of ways to Mark your Display

Move your cursor to the contacts position.

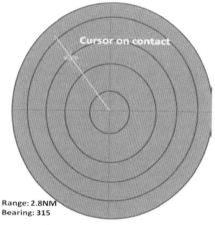

Range: 2.8NM
Bearing: 315

Use your EBL and VRM to Mark

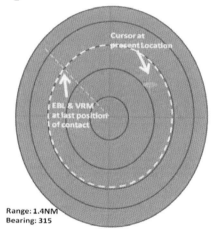

Range: 1.4NM
Bearing: 315

Use a grease pencil to mark the Contact on the display.

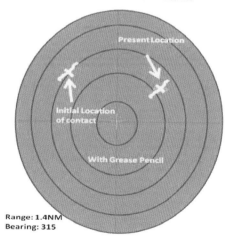

Range: 1.4NM
Bearing: 315

When is CPA Going to Happen

Most of the time, it is not necessary to know when the CPA will occur.

Knowing where the CPA will occur may be all you ever need to be safe. However, sometimes when there are a few contacts it might be nice to know when CPA will occur in order to change course to avoid other contacts.

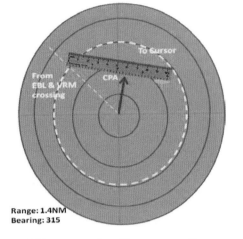

Range: 1.4NM
Bearing: 315

You may use the same two points you used to determine the CPA location to calculate the time the CPA will occur.   The difference in distance of the two marks you made to find the CPA is the distance traveled in a time that equals the difference between the times of the first and second marks.

Speed = Distance/time
Where:
- Speed is in hours
- Distance is in Nautical Miles (NM)
- Time is in Hours

To calculate the speed you may need to convert the distance from yards to miles and the time from minutes to hours.

NM = Distance in yards/2000

Time = Time in Minutes/60

Finding the Time of CPA

1. Note the time with the points used to determine the CPA.
2. The time difference or delta time is the last time point used for locating the CPA minus the first time point used.
3. Measure the distance between the last point and the first points used to determine the CPA.
   a. If using a ruler, note the difference in length.
   b. If using paper, mark the two locations.

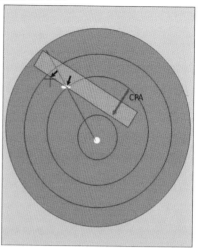

4. Measure the distance in Nautical Miles from the center of the display to the mark on the paper or the length of distance on the ruler noted in step 3. See example to right it is approximately 2NM using the range rings.
5. Speed is distance divided by time in hours.
6. Your measurement is probably in minutes so to calculate the time in hours use the steps below.
   a. 1 hour = 60 minutes
   b. Convert the time to hours by dividing the time difference from step 2 by 60.

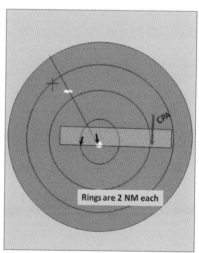

7. The distance must be in Nautical Miles to determine the speed, so if the distance measured is in yards convert to nautical miles as follows.
   a. 1 NM = 2000 Yards
   b. Divide the yards obtained in step 4 by 2000.

8. The relative speed of the contact is then equal to: Distance measured in miles divided by time in hours.

9. Next determine how long it will take the contact to travel from our last mark to the CPA point you determined.

   a. Again find this distance by measuring the distance with a ruler or mark on paper from the last point to the CPA.

   b. Then move the ruler or paper to the center again to determine the number of nautical miles between the two points. See example above. CPA is two range rings out or approximately four nautical miles.

   c. Marking all three points initially, as in the example pictures above, will allow you to do both distances at the same time.

10. The time to CPA will be the distance to CPA divided by the relative speed we found in step 8.

11. The time in step 10 will be in hours so convert it back to minutes by multiplying times 60.

   a. 1 hour = 60 minutes.

   b. Hours from step 10 times 60 to obtain minutes.

12. Now just add the time from step 11 above to the time of the last point time and that will be the time of CPA and you will know when CPA will occur.

The following examples will take you through the process with numbers and should clarify the process.

Examples of CPA Range and Bearing

We have a contact noted at approximately 4 miles out at 1000. The contact is at bearing 313 degrees.

Three minutes later the contact is now at bearing 318 degrees and has now moved into approximately the 3 mile point.

If we lay our straight edge out we find the CPA is approximately one mile away at approximately a bearing of 020.

Now that we know the other vessel will not be less than a mile away when it passes, we can calculate the approximate time that CPA will occur.

1. Determine the difference in time between points used to measure the contacts CPA. In this case:
   a. 1003 – 1000 = 3 minutes

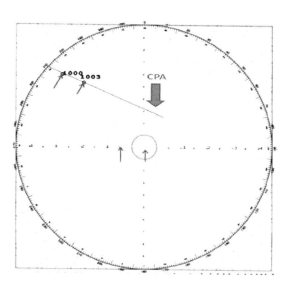

2. Measure the distance between the two points with your ruler or even just a piece of paper.
3. Move the paper to the center and determine the distance traveled.
   a. In this case it is approximately ½ a mile or 1000 yards.
4. Since we used a delta of three minutes, we could apply the three minute rule in reverse.
   a. 1000/100 = 10 knots. (Remember this is a relative speed and is made up of your speed and the contacts speed.)
5. We could have also calculated the speed the long way by time and distance (but I like the 3 minute rule):
   a. 3/60 = .05 hours
   b. .5 miles/.05 hours = 10 Knots

6. To determine when CPA will occur, measure the distance to the CPA with the paper or ruler and then bring it back to the base line again.

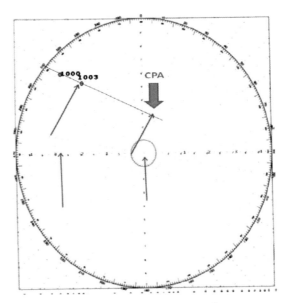

   a. The distance is approximately 2.8 NM.

7. Since the relative velocity between your vessel and the contact vessel is 10 knots, we can divide the remaining distance by the speed to see how much time will pass before the contact will take to travel to the CPA, 2.8 NM from the last point marked.

   a. Time = Distance/Speed
   b. So 2.8NM/10 Knots = 0.28 hours

8. To calculate the time of CPA we now need to calculate the time in minutes and add that time to the 1003 time of the last point.

   a. To convert time in hours to time in minutes = Time in hours * 60
   b. So 0.28 hrs * 60 = 16.8 minutes

9. Now add the time remaining to the last point's time.

   a. Time of CPA = 1003 + 16.8 minutes = 1019.8

10. The CPA will occur at approximately 1020.

When another vessel is a long distance away it is difficult to tell if it is going to run over you or pass a mile away. It is important that you determine the closest point of approach (CPA) for each vessel you are tracking in the fog or even in the daytime.

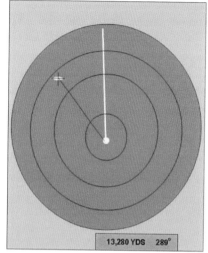

13,280 YDS   289°

Since radar typically provides a relative speed and direction of contact vessels, you can rough out a vector right on the radar display to determine when another vessel will be at its closest point to your vessel or more appropriately the CPA.

A CPA Check Process

1. When we obtain a trace of another ship, run your cursor out to the location of that ship as a marker. Note the cursor bearing and range digital readout indicate the contact is at 13,280 Yards at relative bearing 289°. Since 2000 Yards is approximately one nautical mile, the contact is a bit over 6 ½ miles away. Note: The range rings are at 5,000 yards per ring and the maximum range should then be 15,000 yards or 7.5 Nautical Miles. Get a feel for the numbers whenever you look at the display. (There is no need to panic right now, for the contact is a long way off.)

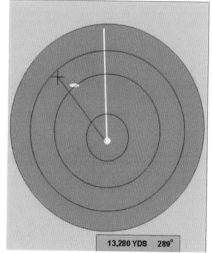

13,280 YDS   289°

2. Exactly five minutes later we check our contact again and find out she is getting closer and headed in front of us. Do we panic now? Not yet! Let's run a line from our cursor through the contact past our vessel.

3. According to our line the contact coming towards us will pass in front of us over 6,000 yards away and be to our starboard at a slightly less distance for CPA. (If neither of us changes speed or course.)
   a. How far?
   b. 6000 yards/ 2000 yards is three nautical miles away.
   c. If the visibility is not good, we might not even see the other vessel.

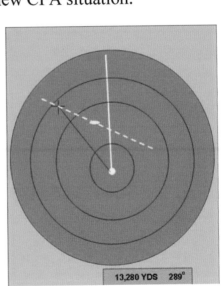

13,280 YDS   289°

4. Continue verifying the track the other ship is on and if you maintain the course you are on, there will be no surprises.
5. In five or six minutes, the contact will be approximately at CPA. After passing CPA keep a watch to make sure the contact does not turn around. Often fishing vessels at sea will go back and forth over a particular area and present a new CPA situation.
6. If you would like to have more room between you and the contact, you can do one or both of two things. Slow your vessel and/or turn to the left. Either of these options will result in the contact passing farther away.
7. Remember the speed and coarse you are tracking is really a combination of your speed and the other vessel's speed.
   a. If you were to turn right it will take longer for the other

13,280 YDS   289°

vessel to pass CPA. However, the CPA would be closer to your vessel.

  b. Turning left will cause the CPA to be farther away, but sooner.

One more CPA Example

If you have Maneuvering board paper, you can plot your contact on the paper. Plotting on graph paper can be a more accurate method, but also more time consuming.   I like to use the display method above, but it may improve your understanding of the concept of CPA by going through a few Maneuvering board type solutions.

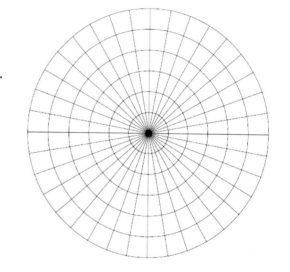

No paper?
Download the Graph Paper program (Graphpap).

http://www.keepandshare.com/doc/181771/graphpap-zip-september-25-2007-8-33-pm-292k

Set up program and then select:

Paper Type: Polar Paper
Scale: N Divided
Divisions: 6 (Press Apply)
Polar Scale Divisions: 10 Degrees

There is also a sample of Graphpap paper in Appendix III as well as one I have marked up with 10 degree steps around the plot you can use or copy and use to play with CPAs. (There are a lot of different plotted paper styles in this program. Some of the other styles may also be useful for other things where you might need a special paper.)

Exercise to find CPA on Polar Paper
As an exercise to see if you understand how to find a CPA, plot the points below on the polar graph paper. After the points are plotter, find the CPA for the contact.

Note the scale for this plot is 10 degree increments around the chart and each circle line represents increments of two miles. (From the center 2, 4, 6, 8, 10, 12 miles)

    We have plotted the first two points:
    1. 10:00 AM – 8 miles @ bearing 098°
    2. 10:18 AM – 6 miles @ bearing 088°

Answer
The answer to the above problem can be found on the plot in Appendix IV. The CPA is approximately: 4.1 NM at 045 degrees.

To find the time of CPA
Measure the relative speed by determining the amount of travel in the 18 minutes specified in the example. Note: 18 minutes is equal to six, 3 minutes periods. The distance traveled measures 2.5 NM. So we will travel 5000 yards in 18 minutes. From the 3 minute rule we can divide the 5000 by 100 (in effect subtract 2 zeros).

    5000/100 = 50

Then since we have 6 periods of 3 minutes the relative speed would then be:

$$50/6 = 8.33 \text{ knots.}$$

(You can also calculate the speed as shown before using speed is equal to distance over time. But I like the 3 minute rule in the cockpit.)

Answer

The distance to CPA from our last point is 4 NM.

So at 8.33 knots it will take: $4nm/8.33 \text{ knots} = .48 \text{ hours}$

or approximately 29 minutes from the last point at 10:18 AM.

CPA will be at $10:18 + 29 = 10:47$ AM.

Changing CPA

After a visual inspection of the CPA we found that we have plenty of space between us and the contact for safe passage. However, if we wanted more space, we could slow our vessel or turn left.

> Speeding up or turning right would decrease the distance at CPA.

Side Note

Rounding the numbers to make the math simple is a good idea as long as you are dealing with enough room to make sure you are not going to have a collision. E.g. Even using a wide grease pencil on the radar display will get you close enough to let you know if you need to take evasive action.

Another CPA Exercise

Obtain a CPA using the polar graph paper again. Plot the points to determine the CPA. Note the scale again is 10 degree increments around the plot and each line circle on the chart represents two mile increments.

We have plotted the first two points:
3. 12:03 PM – 8 miles @ bearing 059°
4. 12:15 PM – 6 miles @ bearing 065°

Answer

The polar plot may be found in Appendix IV. The CPA is approximately: 2.4 NM at 134 degrees.

CPA Time Exercise

Find the time of CPA for the prior CPA solution.

Answer

To find the time of CPA, again measure the relative speed by determining the amount of travel in the 12 minutes of travel between the two points above. The distance traveled measures 2.5 NM. That is 5000 yards in 12 minutes or 4 periods of 3 minutes. From the 3 minute rule we get 50 by dividing by 100. Then since we have 4 periods, the relative speed is then:

50/4 = 12.5 knots.

The distance to CPA from our last point is measured at 5.8 NM. So at 12.5 knots it will take:

5.8 NM/12.5 knots = 0.464 hours

or approximately 28 minutes from the last point at 12:15 PM. CPA will be at 12:15 + 28 = 12:43 PM.

Paper maneuvering board paper or the polar plot paper work well to plot radar contacts. You can also determine the contact's true speed and course using the Maneuvering board paper. However, to avoid contacts, the appropriate action may be taken with relative information only.

It may be very difficult to sail, watch the radar and run a Maneuvering Board while single handing. So using the straight edge, your cursor and the VRM and EBL controls as in the first example will be the fastest way to determine if a contact presents an issue or not.

True Contact Speed and Direction

Before starting this section, it should be noted that when you are cruising you may never have to use this calculation as relative bearing and speed will make sure you do not have a collision.

However, I would be negligent not to cover the process of finding true speed and course in this book. For those that love calculations and trigonometry this will be fun.

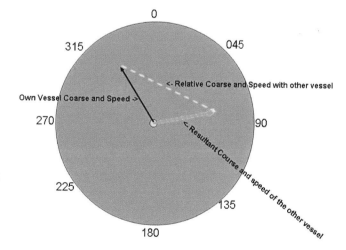

Basic Concept

From relative course and speed, and knowing your course and speed, you can plot those vectors on a maneuvering board plot using the nautical mile and bearings on the plot. Then you may determine the resultant vector, which is the contact's true course and speed.

A Look at how Vector addition works

If you are familiar with vector addition, true speed calculations will be old hat. If it is the first time you have seen it, it may not be all that intuitive.

The basic concept used above is that if you know the speed vector (direction and speed) of two objects you may add them together by adding the vector arrows to establish a resultant direction and speed.

Example

If I am going north at 6 knots and East at 6 knots, the resultant vector of my travel is 045 degrees at approximately 8.5 knots.

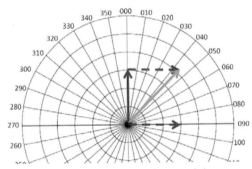

Vector Analysis

To determine true speed of another contact we are starting with two known vectors. The two vectors we know are our own vector (course and speed) and the resultant vector of the two vessels (Relative motion course and speed of the contact).

To determine the true speed of the contact we need to subtract our vessel's speed vector from the relative motion vector. The resultant is the contacts true speed vector.

Example

If I know my resultant speed is 8.5 knots at 045 degrees and my speed at 090 is 6 knots, I can subtract the north vector from the resultant vector to find my easterly travel at 6 knots also by placing the resultant arrow on the known speed and distance. The vector back to the center is the other vector that made up the resultant vector.

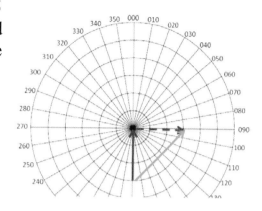

Steps to determine True Speed and Course of a Contact

An example of a vector solution for the other ship's true course and speed calculations are shown in the adjacent figure. The steps below are based on a prior CPA solution in an earlier section of this book.

Example

1. Plot the relative movement of the other vessel on paper with times of plotted range and bearing as before.
2. Plot own vessel's true course and speed with an arrow proportional to your speed and in the direction you are headed.
3. Draw our own vessel's speed vector line

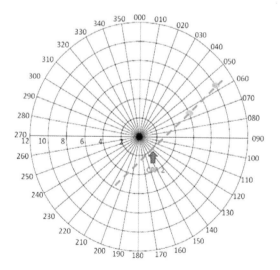

a. For this example, a solid red line is used. Our vessel is shown with a heading of 320 degrees and traveling at a constant speed of 4 knots.

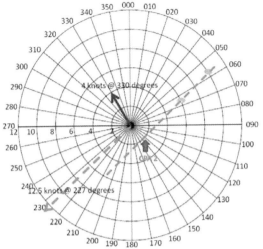

b. The vector line should be drawn in the direction of 320 degrees and out two rings to the 4 NM distance.

4. Determine the relative speed of the other vessel.
   a. We calculated the relative speed to be at 12.5 knots in the prior CPA example.

5. Draw a vector in the direction of relative motion proportional to the relative speed as calculated.
   a. This line should be parallel to the relative motion line with an arrow showing the direction of movement. If you have parallel dividers, use that tool to assure you maintain the angles.
   b. The arrow should be placed at the relative speed end point.
   c. So using our last plotted example, 12.5 knots at an angle of 227 degrees. The speed vector line is shown here as a green dashed line similar to

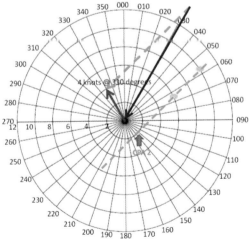

the relative motion line.

6. Now move the contacts relative motion speed vector to the end of your own vessel's speed vector Arrow to Arrow.
   a. Maintain the same angle and length when moving the line. You can use the parallel dividers again to assure the vector is moved properly.

7. Draw a new vector from the end of the relative vector back to the center of the paper (Relative speed vector Green dashed). (Resultant vector is shown as a solid Blue line on the graphic.)

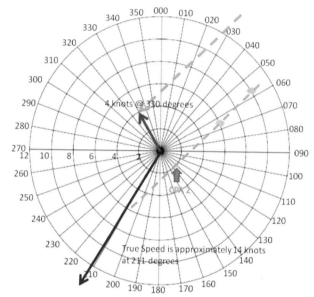

8. The new vector is the actual speed and direction vector of the contact. When you move the tail of the arrow to the center of the plot you can now read off the actual speed and direction of the contact.
   a. Approximately 14 knots at 211 degrees

Chapter 7 – Navigation with Radar

Basic Navigation for Cruisers

GPS provides us with very accurate calculation for our position, direction of travel and speed of travel. As a good safe cruiser it is always important to have a backup plan to make sure you make it home. What to do in the event it is dark, there is fog, etc., and the GPS dies. This may not be your GPS, but it could be the system being shut down as a result of world activity.

The first time my GPS died I was only marginally prepared. It was total darkness and I was headed for a harbor for the first time I had not planned on stopping at. This can be real exciting. My survival and safe entry into the dark port became dependent on my charts and radar. I guess we made it, but it was an adventure.

Recommendations
Either plot your position/fixes on a paper chart or keep a log of positions on a frequent basis as I do so that you could plot on a chart the dead reckoning and position data after the loss of GPS. Back up GPS units are fine, but it is very possible that the GPS could be turned off after a world event. The position fixes will allow you to correct for your dead reckoning plot of speed and course. You can then calculate the set and drift based on the position fixes from the GPS. Then if the GPS dies, you just don't have a fix for a while. I would suspect that less than 10% of the cruisers today keep track of their position on any form of paper or have area charts on board to allow them to utilize this method. GPS charts and displays make it far too easy to navigate and we all get a bit lax at what we really should be doing.

Today's GPS technology is so good and the chart plotters add so much value that even the US Navy is moving toward paperless charts. Don't forget though that the Navy will have expensive professional grade redundant systems and more staff than any of us cruisers.

Radar navigation is provided in this book to help you stay out of trouble. It is recommended that vessel captains try navigating a few times to establish a backup method of navigation.

1. Have the paper charts on board and be familiar with them for the area you plan to travel.
2. Keep a log that identifies your GPS position, Speed Over Ground (SOG), Course Over Ground (COG), compass heading, and boat speed.
3. Take log readings at least every hour in case the GPS dies. The logic is that I can plot the latest data in the log onto my charts within a few minutes.
4. If the GPS fails, maintain your last logged compass heading. That heading should keep you on the same course the GPS wanted you on. The GPS course automatically compensated for any set and/or drift that might have been present. The GPS had you traveling directly to the next waypoint on a course compensating for the set and drift.
5. Plot your last position fix and a dead reckoning line based on logged heading.
6. You can also establish a GPS heading line to compare the heading line to the GPS course. You should then have some idea how much set and drift were at the time you lost your GPS.
7. Eventually you will need more position fixes to update the set and drift.
8. Keeping track of the time traveled and the speed will be a dead reckoned position on the plotted line(s).

Obtaining your location with Radar and charts

For coastal, river, and lake sailing, you can take bearings and/or ranges to points of land, towers, etc. that are shown on your charts. The point at where the bearings cross is where you are. A radar position fix is clearly not as accurate as a GPS position fix, but they are good fixes. The main reason for the decrease in accuracy is our inability to precisely locate the points we are measuring our position fix from. E.g. points of land, towers etc. However, a radar fix can get your boat home or into a new port if the GPS dies or you don't even have a GPS.

First Checking the Radar's Bearing Accuracy
Make sure you have verified the bearing accuracy to assure that 000 degrees relative bearing is actually 000 degrees. That means the radar antenna was mounted on your boat correctly before using the radar for bearing fixes. Range fixes should always be accurate.

1. Check your radar's alignment; while in port find a tower, a point of land or something you can identify on your radar display. Read a few ranges and bearing points to several; targets.

2. Note your boats location and heading in the slip on your chart.

3. Determine the range and bearing to each object you have selected.

4. Your radar bearings are in relative bearing, so you will need to add/subtract out your vessel's heading.

5. Your bearings are to the target so the measured bearings to the target must be inverted to use the target as a reference. That means you must take the reciprocal of the bearing from your radar. Big words, just subtract 180 degrees to get the reciprocal. See table below that provides an example of manipulating the numbers to establish the proper bearings.

From our targets we then get

$$MB = RB + MH +/- 180$$

Own Ships Magnetic Heading	target Range NM	target Relative Bearing	target Magnetic Bearing	Reciprocal +/- 180 depending on value
357	4.44	17.1	374.1	194.1
357	3.91	64.3	421.3	241.3
OR	Subtracting 360 degrees		14.1	194.1
	Subtracting 360 degrees		61.3	241.3

Range and Bearing Fixes

You can use you radar to obtain a range(s) and/or bearing(s) to a known point to yield your position. A position fix may be found by getting two bearings to different objects or two ranges to different objects and then identifying where the plotted lines or arcs cross on your chart. Since you are probably moving when you are getting a position fix, be sure take reading quickly and record the time of the position fixes to help you weigh the actual position at a specific time.

Taking more position fixes and using ranges and bearings together to two objects will increase your position fix accuracy. Taking two ranges and bearings provides effectively 4 fixes. Two measurements to two different points provides the following fix references: Range plus range, range plus bearing 1, range plus bearing 2, and bearing 1 plus bearing 2.

A simple two points bearing fix.

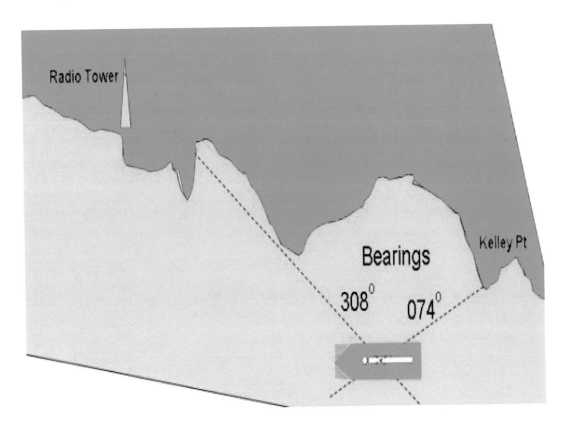

When two range and bearing fixes plotted together they will provide the four position fixes and can significantly improve the accuracy of your fix by finding the center of all plotted data. The two range and bearings do need to be obtained quickly (close together) with an accurate time for each range and bearing for the best results.

If your radar as VRM and EBL features, you can track a point and get near constant position fixes from the EBL and VRM display readouts each time you re-adjust for your position change.

Plotting on your Chart

For Ranges: Use a compass to establish the distance measured by a radar range. Measure each range on the chart drawing a small ark near where you think you might be from the targeted fix reference point. When two ranges are plotted the point where the arcs cross is a position fix.

For Bearings: Draw a small line, based on the reciprocal line from the targeted fix reference point at approximately where you think your vessel is located. (A reciprocal line is a line 180 degrees from the line found on the radar. In other words the angle from the target being used for the position fix to your boat.) The picture below shows a solid line from each reference point. Note: Only a short line near where you think you are located, as with the arcs for range plots, are necessary to obtain the fix crossing points.

Where the lines cross or group is a great position fix. Again the bearing and ranges provide four possible fixes thus improving the accuracy of the position fix.

When you travel beyond the sight of land, there may not be any reference points from which to obtain radar position fixes. Be creative though when you are close enough to see shorelines, buoys mountains, towers, etc.

You can use radio towers, buoys, points of land, and basically anything you can see on your chart and on the radar as position/fix reference points.

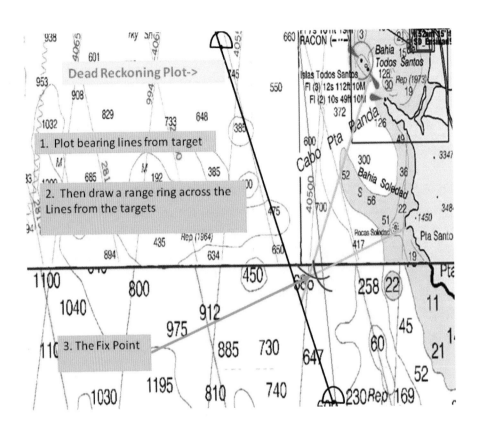

Chapter 8 – Radar Interference

Interference from other radars can present very interesting displays. Some displays will develop spots all over the radar display. Not realizing it is interference from other radar(s) can result in operators thinking their radar is not working.

What is Interference

Our cruising radars operate on approximately the same frequency. If you go back to the basics, our radar transmits then listens for a long time.

When we are close to another vessel operating their radar, instead of just the echoes from our radar, we may get strong signals coming in from the other radar.

Our radar does not know where the received signal is coming from but displays the signals received.

The waveform on our display will vary a lot depending on how far way the other radar is and how close to our frequency the other radar is. When we tune our radar, or have it in automatic tuning, it tunes the receiver to the transmit frequency. Even though our transmit frequency will change slightly, while in automatic tuning the receiver will stay locked on our transmit frequency. The other radar is probably doing the same thing. However both transmitted frequencies are changing slightly over time and can result in some interesting displays as they pass through each other's tuned frequencies.

What does Interference Look Like?

Inside a marina interference can often occur. Interference on your radar may be the first thing you see when you are in range of a new contact out at sea.

Sometimes the display may look like a flower of dashed lines and sometimes it may look like contacts all the way around you.

This interference type looks a bit like flowers around the screen. It may not be as distinct as this, but you will see lots of dots.

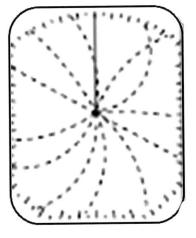

Another common occurrence is the ring around your boat. The ring will change in intensity and may even blank out your screen.

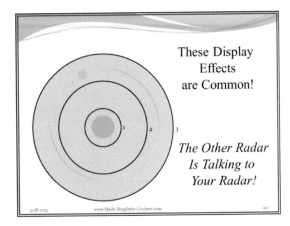

These Display
Effects
are Common!

*The Other Radar
Is Talking to
Your Radar!*

Chapter 9 – AIS

While AIS **in no way replaces radar**, it can provide some of the similar information to allow you to automatically determine CPA from position information being transmitted by the other vessel.

Many cruisers use active AIS and transmit their position and other information hoping that others will read the information and stay out of their way. There are some good reasons to use active AIS instead of receive only AIS, but this is not one of the reasons.

AIS can be helpful and calculate the CPA time and distance between vessels based on the data received from the other vessel and your ships GPS data. Normally this data will be very accurate, but if either vessel has problems with their GPS, it would result in incorrect or no solutions on your AIS display.

For some reason the AIS standard does not include CPA bearing. When a vessel is coming toward you, you may see CPA at 20 yards in 20 minutes on your display. Without the bearing information and radar the contact could be crossing your bow or keeping to the left by 20 yards. This is an unfortunate oversight in my opinion on the part of the IMO standard as in order to calculate time and distance, the angle was also calculated, but not displayed. To compensate for this lack of information, I have found that making a small course change to the right will either open or close the distance to the contact at CPA. If the contact will be closer at CPA I then make a significant course correction to the left to assure at least 100 yard or greater separation. Even if I have the right of way on paper I always figure size counts…

Normally the AIS system receives actual speed, course, and Latitude and Longitude information from the other vessels. So the CPA information should be very accurate.

Even with AIS on board, you should practice obtaining CPA and comparing it to the AIS calculated CPA so you are ready for those vessels without AIS transmitters.

The best part of AIS for me is that AIS provides vessel names. When you call a large vessel by their name, they may answer back. Without a name, unfortunately they seem to ignore us little cruisers.

Another tip when trying to contact a large vessel to establish your passing plans, use your Digital Selective Calling (DSC) to contact them. AIS will provide you with the Maritime Mobile Service Identity (MMSI) number. Plugging the MMSI number into your VHF radio DSC function and establishing a call on VHF channel 13 will significantly increase the chance the commercial vessel will answer back as it results in an alarm on the bridge the officer of the deck is sure to hear.

Appendix I – Radar Types

Analog Radar

Traditional radar that puts out a pulse and via receiver and amplifiers displays the returned energy to a display device.

Digital Radar

Digital radar is similar to Analog radar except the returned signal is put into a digital format so that it may be colorized as to strength and overlaid onto a GPS charts.

The displayed radar information may follow the GPS displayed data.
1. That is when true or magnetic north is selected the radar will overlay in true or magnetic north.
2. If the GPS display is in relative or heading up, the radar will be normal in relative bearing mode.
3. So be careful to always know which way is up. . . . .
   .

Broadband Radar

Broadband radar is the newest technology in radar and actually puts out a lower power frequency sweeping signal. The frequency and rate of change is known to the radar's computer. When the reflected signal is returned, the target range is basically calculated based on when that specific frequency left the transmitter and the time it took to return to the receiver.

Adding changes in frequency to the time elapsed for the returned signal adds an additional dimension to the displayed data and increases the definition of the targets. This radar is said to be a very good short range/harbor solution, but not typically recommended for used in long range for vessels at sea.

Appendix II – Radar Manufactures

Just a few standard cruising radars typically sold and used by cruisers in the US.

- Raymarine
- Garmin
- Simrad
- Furuno
- Loranz

Appendix III – Polar Chart Paper

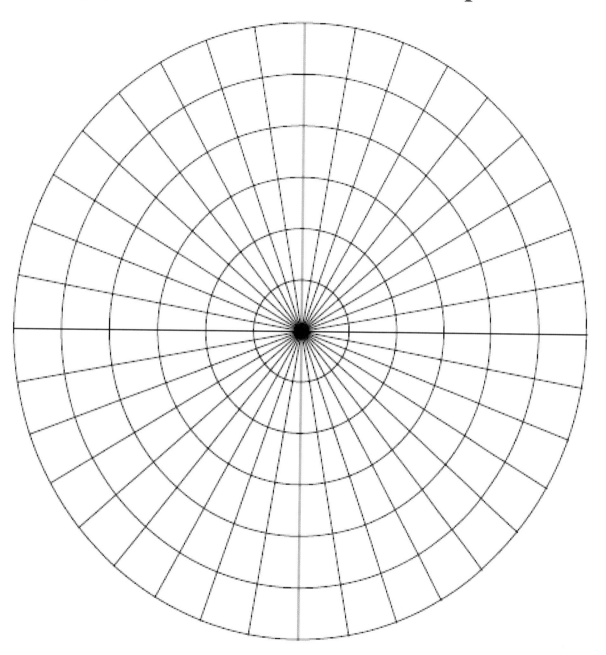

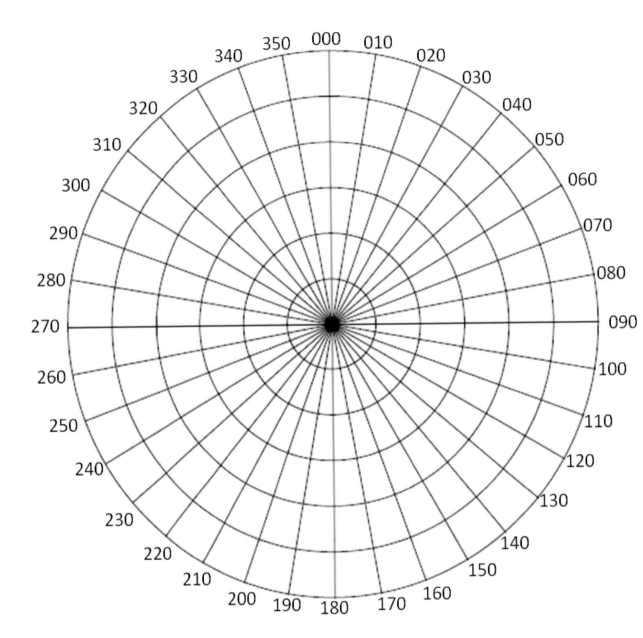

Page 92

Appendix IV – Plots for CPA Questions

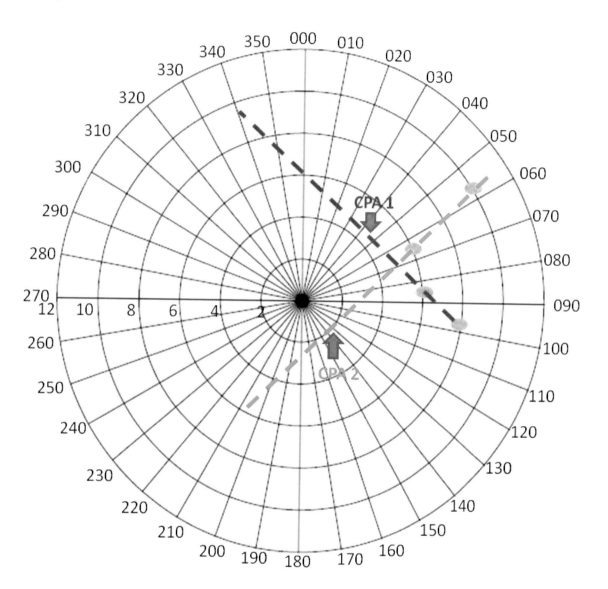

KISS Dictionary

Airmail – PC Software used for both Sailmail and Winlink email systems. The Sailmail and Winlink versions are slightly different, but may run together on the same computer. The Airmail program was written by Jim Corenman.

AIS – Automated Identification System. AIS information is broadcast on two frequencies within the VHF marine radio spectrum.

Amateur HF Band Frequencies – The FCC has allocated specific frequencies within the HF band to radio amateur. To transmit on these frequencies you must pass exams for Technician and General Class Amateur. It is illegal in all countries to transmit on these channels as they are also controlled internationally by the ITU. (Except in an emergency)

The frequencies within the Amateur radio:

1.8MHZ to 2MHz (MHF band)	160 Meter Band – LSB
3.5MHZ to 4MHz	80 Meter Band – LSB
5.3305MHz to 5.4035MHz – 50 watts maximum	60 Meter Band – USB
7MHz to7.3MHZ	40 Meter Band – LSB
10.1MHz to 10.15MHz RTTY/Data	30 Meter Band –
14MHz to 14.35MHz USB	20 Meter Band –
18.068MHz to 18.168MHz USB	17 Meter Band –
21.025MHz to 21.45MHz USB	15 Meter Band –
24.89MHz to 24.99MHz	12 Meter Band – USB
28MHz to 29.7MHz USB	10 Meter Band –

Amateur Packet Radio – Communications over Amateur radio between two computers.

Amplitude – The level of voltage or current for audio or radio frequencies.

Amplitude Modulation – "AM" contains a carrier frequency (the one you tune to receive the signal) and "intelligence" in the Upper Sideband, Lower Sidebands.

Ampere – Unit used to measure current flow and uses the symbol I. I = Voltage/Resistance

AF – Audio Frequency. The Audio frequency band is 20Hz to 20,000Hz, but most of us old guys only make it to about 10-12,000Hz. Most dogs hear the 20,000Hz fine.

Analog – Continuous voltage levels that may change gradually or rapidly as opposed to digital that changes from a one to a zero and back near instantaneously. An analog reading of a voltage tells us what the voltage is. Depending on the resolution it take 8, 16, or, 32 bits in digital to define the analog voltage measured.

Antenna – A device or structure used to receive to transmit electromagnetic waves.

Band – A group of frequencies. Similar to the AM band and FM band the HF Band includes all the frequencies from 3MHz to 30MHz.

Bandwidth – The frequencies that are allowed to come into the radio above and below the radio's tuned frequency. If the radio is tuned at 1,000 kHz, but it will allow 9980 kHz up to 1,020 kHz the radio would have a 40 kHz Bandwidth.

Baud – Baud is the number of bits per second transmitted.

Baud Rate – Baud rate is the measure of for serial communications such as with a modem.

Bits per second bps – BPS is the rate at which bits stream in a serial communication. 300 bps is also 300 baud. If a word is 10 bits, then 300 baud would be 30 characters per second or 30cps.

Bonding –Tying together all major metal items on a boat that extend into the water to control/reduce galvanic corrosion on a boat.

Call Frequency – Are the transmit and receive frequencies that will be used for digital data such as Latitude, longitude, time, MMSI number etc. sent as a Digital Selective Calling (DSC) message or acknowledgements to a DSC message sent by another vessel.

Carrier Signal – Base frequency to which the modulation or intelligence is applied in order to be transmitted. The carrier signal may be modulated using Frequency modulation (FM), Amplitude modulation (AM) or several other forms of applying intelligence to a radio transmittable frequency.

Clarity – Clarity is typically used on Single Sideband radios to adjust the received frequency for better understandability of an incoming signal while the transmitter signal remains on the assigned frequency. Some older radios, may not be transmitting on the exact frequency and as a result the Donald Duck effect from being off frequency may make it hard to understand the other station.

Coaxial Cable – Special cable used to connect two radio frequency devices that contain a center conductor and a mesh cable that completely surrounds the center conductor. Examples: RG8U, RG213, RG58 for Communications and RG59 for TV cable.

CW – Continuous Wave. CW is typically used by Amateur radio operators and others. The carrier frequency, the frequency tuned to on the radio, is turned off and on at a rate representing Morse code. The intelligence is then the carrier turning on and off.

Cycles Per Second – CPS was re-named to Hertz (Hz) many years ago as folks frequently took a short cut and just called it cycles which does not give a time reference. Hz is always CPS.

Counterpoise – Ground side of an antenna system made out of copper strip or mesh. Also referred to as ground plane.

DERA – This is the "DSC Emergency Reception Antenna". As Named by this Author. DERA is a broad frequency range reception antenna that is connected to the antenna 2 position on the IC M802. Without this antenna no Distress calls, acknowledgments, urgent or ships calls will be heard.

DSC – Digital Selective Calling. A digital transmission used to contact other stations in emergencies or just to call a friend making connection without using a hailing channel.

DSC Receiver – A special purpose receiver built into the Icom M802 that monitors Distress frequency transmissions using J2B modulation (digital SSB).

Duplex Communications – Transmission on one frequency with Reception on a different frequency. Duplex frequency communication is typically used for ship to shore communications and most shore stations have a separate transmitter and receiver so you can always here the ship talking.

Email Ready – Marine HF SSB that is capable of sending email. Email requires the transmitter be capable of full power for one or two minutes as the transmitter cycles between receive and transmit. Older analog HF SSB unit were not built to transmit full power for minutes at a time.

Emission – This is another way of saying how the intelligence is applied to the carrier frequency. Common emission types include AM and FM. For SSB, upper and lower sidebands are frequently used. Emission types used by the IC – M802:

- **A1A (CW)** – Double-sideband amplitude modulation (e.g. AM broadcast radio); One channel containing digital information; Aural telegraphy, intended to be decoded by ear, such as Morse code.

- **F1B (FSK)** – FM broadcast radio; One channel containing digital information; Electronic telegraphy, intended to be decoded by machine.

- **H3E** – Single-sideband with full carrier; One channel containing analogue information; Voice or Music intended to be listened to by a human.

- *J2B (Receive Only)* – Single-sideband with suppressed carrier; One channel containing digital information, using a subcarrier; Electronic telegraphy, intended to be decoded by machine.
- *J3E (USB/LSB)* – Single-sideband with suppressed carrier; One channel containing analogue information; Voice or Music intended to be listened to by a human.
- *JB3* – Upper Sideband transmission

EPIRB – Emergency Position Indicating Radio Beacon

Frequency – The number of times a signal goes from zero volts to Max positive volts to zero volts to max negative to zero volts in a period of one second. Cycle per second measured in Hertz.

Frequency Modulation – (FM) is where a carrier frequency, the frequency you tune the radio to, and the carrier frequency changes with the "intelligence". When the transmitted frequency is equal to (and not changing) the carrier frequency, the radio is quiet, "No Intelligence".

Galvanic Corrosion – Corrosion that destroys metal as a result of current flowing between two metal objects usually in water. Two metal objects with saltwater between them forms a small battery. Shorting the two metal objects with wire eliminates any voltage difference and thus current flow.

GMDSS – Global Maritime Distress and Safety System   All Ships over 300 Tons Must have operational and monitored GMDSS equipment on board. The GMDS equipment includes systems to monitors HF and VHF voice and DSC calls for Emergencies of all vessels. GMDSS vessels also have Satellite Equipment on board. Can be Your Link for Safety at Sea!

Ground Wave – A radio signal that travels along the surface of the earth.

Hertz – unit of measure of frequency. One hertz = 1Hz = 1 complete cycle in one second.

HF Email – Email that is sent by your computer to a modem and then the radio. A subscription or Amateur Radio license is required for HF email.

Impedance – The opposition to the flow of current as a result of resistance capacitance and inductance within a circuit.

ITU – International Telecommunications Union based in Geneva, Switzerland. The ITU is the Czar for world communications. Countries input frequency needs and the ITU keeps us all from over running each other.

kHz – Kilo Hertz, is thousands of cycles per second

LSB Transmission – Lower Side Band Transmission. A form of Amplitude modulation where the carrier frequency and the Upper Sideband are eliminated to allow all the power in the radio to be output in the one upper sideband. No power is sent out except when "intelligence" is added through the microphone or modem.

Marine Frequencies Bands – Marine HF SSB bands. Some of the frequencies also include Amateur band, but again, the license is required. [Upper side band (USB) Only]

- 1.6MHz to 2.9999MHz
- 4.0MHz to 4.9999MHz
- 6.0 MHz to 6.9999MHz
- 8.0MHz to 8.9999MHz
- 12.0MHz to 13.9999MHz
- 16.0MHz to 17.9999MHz
- 18.0MHz to 19.9999MHz
- 22.0MHz to 22.9999MHz
- 25.0MHz to 27.5MHz

MHz – Mega Hertz, is millions of cycles per second

MMSI – Maritime Mobile Service Identification number. The MMSI is a unique number around the world. It is assigned by your country and sent to the International Telecommunications Union (ITU) to be entered into an international database used by Search and Rescue (SAR) teams around the world.

Modem – A device connected between your computer and the HF radio that changes the digital signals out of the computer to a signal that can be sent over the HF Band. Pactor modems seem to be the most popular for Cruisers.

Morse Code – Morse Code is a method of communicating by turning the carrier frequency on and off or a modulating tone on and off at a specific rate for marks and spaces. Morse Code requires both the sender and receiver to know the code resulting in intelligence being transferred from one location to another.

NMEA – A signal format that is used to move information via wires from point "A" to point "B". Typical data would include GPS position and time data.

NEMA 0183 Version 3.01 – Is the NMEA connection on the M802 is for some reason a BNC coaxial connector instead of the standard two wire or terminal connections. While this may increase the difficulty of inputting the GPS signal, you can by factory made BNC cables that may be cut and used for this connection. The M802 requires sentence" **GGA**" to be sent to read the GPS.

Pactor – A frequency shift keying mode. Pactor format is used to modulate HF SSB radios using a Pactor modem to send emails.

Pactor Protocol Software – This is the software is used to compress/decompress and modulate/demodulate the transceiver. Pactor 3 protocol is 3 to 4 times faster than Pactor 2 and Pactor 4 is twice that of Pactor 3. The assumption here is that both the email service and the user are utilizing the same level of protocol. If you have a Pactor 4 protocol modem, the modem will also talk to Pactor stations with Pactor 2 and Pactor 3 protocol at the slowest modems in the links speed. Pactor 4 software is claimed to be twice as fast as Pactor 3 software. However this is only when talking to another Pactor 4 unit. The slowest Pactor in the link rules.

Pile Ups – More than one station trying to transmit at the same time and as a result no one is really understood. Usually just a lot of noise.

Propagation Tool – This software tool will help communicators determine what frequency has a chance of linking up with another location. The tool will tell you what will not work and only what might work as the tool only knows basic propagation information and not about cloud cover, local noise and storms that may impact actual communications.

RF Radio Frequency – Frequencies that are made up of electromagnetic energy and may be used to transmit intelligence. RF is generally thought of as high frequency, but there are also transmitters that broadcast in the audio frequency range. They are transmitting electromagnetic waves and not sound waves, so you cannot actually hear the transmission without a receiving device.

Received Signal – A small signal collected on the antenna that is amplified by the radio and turned back into information or intelligence.

R-S-T Signal Reporting – Readability by Signal Strength

    Readability: 1 = unreadable, 2 =Barely readable, 3 = Readable with difficulty, 4 = No difficulty, 5 = Perfect.

    Strength: 1=Faint,2=very week, 3=weak, 4=fair, 5=fairly good, 6=good, 7=moderately strong, 8 strong, 9= very strong   (E.g. "I read you 4 by 6" is readable with a good signal.)

Scan – An automated method of looking at many frequencies, one at a time, to help look for transmitting stations.

Sensitivity – This term applies to how well the receiver portion of the radio can convert the very small received signal into intelligence you can hear in the speaker.

SFI – Solar Flux Index, a factor that is used to help predict the best frequency to use by a Propagation tool.

Simplex Communication – Transition and reception on the same frequency. Simplex is typically used for ship to ship communication. Simplex can also be used to call and communicate with a shore station. If the shore station has a separate transmitter and receiver, duplex frequencies may be established to ensure that the shore facilities will always here the ship station even if they are trying to talk. Transmitting at the same time using simplex will result in neither party hearing the other party.

Single Side Band (SSB) – A transmission mode where the carrier frequency and one of the sidebands are suppressed such that the only energy radiated is contained in one sideband.   SSB can be Upper Sideband (USB) or Lower Sideband (LSB) transmission.

Sky Wave – Radio signals that bounce to and from the Ionosphere and the earth's surface.

Snap on Ferrite Cores – These devices are used around cables to act as a block to RF into a device. Often computer equipment includes ferrite cores that are pre-molded onto the cable.   Cruisers should consider putting ferrite cores on every cable connection for your radio, modem, and computer equipment as well as other devices around the boat that turn on or off when transmitting on HF SSB radio.

Speed of light and radio waves – 300,000,000Meters per second.

Spurious emissions – Unwanted frequencies and that are not within the designed bandwidth of the radio.

Traffic Frequency – Traffic frequencies are the transmitted and the received frequencies that will be used for voice communications. Transmit and receive frequencies will be entered as the same frequency for simplex operation and different for duplex operation.

Transmitted Signal – Is the electromagnetic signal that propagates from the antenna. The radiated signal is created from a large power signal that is fed to the antenna where it creates the electromagnetic field around the antenna and then radiates the signal in to the atmosphere.

Tropospheric Propagation – Also called Tunneling. Tunneling allows signal refraction for frequencies above 30MHz such as VHF radio.   Result from atmospheric conditions such as temperature inversions.

Tuner – The box in between the radio output and the antenna that is responsible for matching the antenna to the transmitter to minimize SWR and maximize radiated power from the antenna.

USB Transmission – Upper Side Band Transmission.   A form of Amplitude modulation where the carrier frequency and the Lower Sideband are eliminated to allow all the power in the radio to be output in the one upper sideband.   No power is sent out except when "intelligence" is added through the microphone or modem.

Standing Wave Ratio (SWR) – SWR is not a good thing. The number represents the amount of power that is sent out of a transmitter to the antenna, but bounces back because of a poor antenna match. High SWR can hurt your radio. The Antenna Tuner is responsible to keep the SWR low, but must have an adequate antenna and ground system to work effectively.   From forward power and reflected power you may calculate SWR.   Under the Communications page on www.made-simplefor-Cruisers.com there is a spread sheet that will allow you to calculate and save SWR history.

Transceiver – A radio that is capable of both transmitting signal and receiving signal capability.

Tuner – An automated device that adjusts the electrical length of an antenna and grounding system to the proper length to match the requirements for the output of a transmitter.

USB – Upper Sideband is used to send intelligence and the lower sideband LSB and carrier are suppressed.

UTC – Universal Coordinated Time. UTC is essentially the same as Greenwich Mean Time. Coordinated Universal Time is a time standard based on an International Atomic Time. UTC is also referred to as Zulu time.

Winlink 2000 – Amateur radio sponsored and supported email service provider.

WL2K – Winlink 2000 is the connecting station for the Amateur email system.

Wave Length – Wave Length is the distance a complete cycle would extend as it is moving away from the source. In the case of the radio transmission it would be the distance the beginning of the cycle has moved, at approximately the speed of light, when the last part of the cycle leaves the transmitter.

Wave Length in meters is = 300/Frequency in MHz.

To transmit energy from an antenna the signal must see at least a ½ wave antenna. This can be made up of the Backstay on a sailboat plus the contribution from the antenna tuner plus the ground plain on the boat. The tuner has the task of making up the difference when the antenna and ground plain are to short or too long.

Zulu – another term frequently used to represent UTC or Greenwich mean time.

Help!

If you need help send me an email at: p-t_on_sunyside@live.com

Downloads and book updates available at:

www.made-simplefor-Cruisers.com

Come Join Us Living the Dream

"Handbooks for Starting the Dream"

Volume 1 – "Cruising Starting from Scratch" 2nd Edition

Volume 2 – "Communications Made Simple for Cruisers" 2nd Edition

Volume 3 – "Icom IC M802 Made Simple for Cruisers" 2nd Edition

Volume 4 – "Radar Made Simple for Cruisers" 2nd Edition

Volume 5 – "Icom IC M802 Starting from Scratch"

Volume 6 – "A New Ham I Am * Made Simple for Cruisers"

34746953R00061

Made in the USA
Charleston, SC
16 October 2014